EXCELLENCE

REVISED EDITION

John W. Gardner

EXCELLENCE

Can We Be Equal and Excellent Too?

REVISED EDITION

W · W · NORTON & COMPANY

New York · London

Published simultaneously in Canada by
Penguin Books Canada Ltd,
2801 John Street, Markham, Ontario L3R 1B4.

The text of this book is composed in Avanta, with display type set in Garamond.
Composition and manufacturing are by the Haddon Craftsmen. Book design is by
Marjorie J. Flock.

Library of Congress Cataloging in Publication Data
Gardner, John William, 1912–
    Excellence: can we be equal and excellent too?
    Revised Edition
    Includes bibliographical references and index.
    1. Equality.   2. Individuality.   3. Leadership.
4. Academic achievement.   I. Title.
HM146.G29   1984   305   83-25070

ISBN 0-393-01848-2

W. W. Norton & Company, Inc., 500 Fifth Avenue, New York, N. Y. 10110
W. W. Norton & Company Ltd., 37 Great Russell Street, London WC1B 3NU

    4 5 6 7 8 9 0

To my mother and brother

Contents

8   *Contents*

Introduction

THE ORIGINAL EDITION of *Excellence* was published in 1961 and sold steadily for twenty-two years. When the question of a revised edition came up, I had the wholly mistaken notion that it could be freshened up with a new foreword and minor editing throughout.

It didn't work. The twenty-two years since first publication had been more than ordinarily eventful—eventful for the world and for me. There were new things to write about and I felt impelled to discuss even the older topics in new ways. None of the major theses in the original book has been shaken by time. But my own temperament—to say nothing of two decades of active living—would not permit me to move comfortably along the tracks I had laid down two decades earlier.

I have tried to keep as much of the original material as possible but have rewritten it freely and have added new chapters and sections.

Some things remain the same. This is a book about excellence, more particularly about the conditions under which excellence is possible in our kind of society; but it also deals, necessarily, with some of the questions surrounding the concept of equality, the kinds of equality that can and must be honored, and the kinds that cannot be forced.

Such a book must raise questions that Americans have shown little inclination to discuss rationally.

What are the characteristic difficulties a democracy encounters in pursuing excellence? Is there a way out of these difficulties?

How equal do we want to be? How equal can we be?

Can an equalitarian society tolerate winners? On what terms?

Have the schools failed to train our youngsters for the complex technological world they will have to live in?

Does every young American have a "right" to a college education?

Are we headed toward domination by an intellectual elite?

Is it possible for a people to achieve excellence if they don't believe in anything? Have the American people lost their sense of purpose and the drive that would make it possible for them to achieve excellence?

I have discussed these matters with a great variety of individuals and groups throughout the country, and I find that "excellence" is a curiously powerful word—a word about which people feel strongly and deeply. But it is a word that means different things to different people. It is a little like those ink blots that psychologists use to interpret personality. As we contemplate the word "excellence" we read into it our own aspirations, our own conception of high standards, our hopes for a better world. And it brings powerfully to our minds evidence of the betrayal of excellence (as we conceive it). We think not only of the greatness we might achieve but of the mediocrity we have fallen into. Reactions to the word "excellence" are so numerous and diverse that they create difficulties for the writer concerned with the topic. When one has had his say, someone is certain to mutter, "How could he talk about excellence without mentioning the Greeks?" And another, "He didn't say a word about the plight of the artist." . . . "Nor teachers' salaries." . . . "Nor the evils of bureaucracy."

It isn't just that people have different opinions about excellence. They see it from different vantage points. The elementary school teacher preoccupied with instilling respect for standards in seven-year-olds will think about it in one way. The literary critic concerned with understanding and interpreting the highest reaches of creative expression will think of it in a wholly different way. The executive, the composer, the intellectual historian—each will raise a different set of questions and arrive at different answers.

It may help the reader to know what my own vantage point is. I am concerned with the social context in which excellence may survive or be smothered. I am concerned with the fate of excellence in our society. This preoccupation may lead me to neglect some of the interesting and perplexing problems of excellence as these confront the specialist striving for the highest reaches of performance in a particular field. I am sorry that such neglect must occur, but I leave its repair to other writers. This book is concerned with the difficult, puzzling, delicate, and important business of toning up a whole society, of bringing a whole people to that fine edge of morale and conviction and zest that makes for greatness.

This is not a Utopian tract. Some of those who complain

about the quality of our national life seem to be dreaming of a world in which everyone without exception has talent, taste, judgment, and an unswerving allegiance to excellence. Such dreams are pleasant but unprofitable. The problem is to achieve some measure of excellence *in this society*, with all its beloved and exasperating clutter, with all its exciting and debilitating confusion of standards, with all the stubborn problems that won't be solved and the equally stubborn ones that might be.

Some aspects of excellence have been the subject of extensive and authoritative treatment. The whole field of literary criticism, for example, may be regarded as one long exercise in appraising, understanding, defining, and savoring excellence in one important area of human activity. But the subject with which I shall deal has received relatively little attention. And this is not surprising, because it involves complex and controversial social issues, some of which Americans find it embarrassing to talk about.

This book deals with only one of the many problems facing our society. But it is a problem that cuts across all the others. If a society cannot rouse itself to the pursuit of excellence, the consequences will be felt in everything that it undertakes. The disease may not attack every organ, but the resulting debility will be felt in all parts of the system. Everything that it does and everything that it strives for will be affected.[1]*

*Superior numbers refer to a section of notes beginning on page 165.

Excellence

CHAPTER ONE

The Decline of Hereditary Privilege

You Can Keep a Good Man Down

IF WE ACCEPT the common usage of words, nothing can be more readily disproved than the old saw, You can't keep a good man down. Most human societies of which we have any historical record have been beautifully organized to keep good men and women down. The reasons are many, but the most obvious is that throughout most of recorded history societies of hereditary privilege have predominated.

In such societies the individual's status was determined not by gifts or capacities but by membership in a family, caste, or class. Such membership determined the individual's rights, privileges, prestige, power, and status in the society. Status was not earned.

The faithful family servant of scores of Victorian novels described one aspect of such a society by saying, "I know my place." And Molly Malone—who was part of such an order—sang, "My father and mother were fishmongers too." Birth determined occupation and status. It determined whom you bowed to, who bowed to you, the weight of your voice in the community, and the kinds of suitors who sought your daughter's hand.

Such societies were doomed by the Industrial Revolution. It was essential to the new modes of economic organization that individuals be free to bargain (and be bargained for) in the open market on the basis of their capacity to perform. A corporation, for example, requires among other things flexible movement and interchange of people *on the basis of their usefulness to the organization.* This is impossible in a society that determines status on the basis of relationship. One doesn't give the Prince of Wales an aptitude test and start him in the stock room.

But the Industrial Revolution was not the only factor in bringing a new measure of autonomy to the individual. The seventeenth and eighteenth centuries had seen the emergence of religious ideas that laid great stress on individual responsibility. Tawney remarked of the Puritan that he was a natural republican, "for there is none on earth that he can own as master."[1] And eighteenth-century ideas of democracy demanded that the individual be allowed to function politically regardless of hereditary status. Thomas Jefferson, borrowing a vivid phrase from an English revolutionary, said, " . . . the mass of mankind has not been born with saddles on their backs, nor a favored few booted and spurred, ready to ride them legitimately, by the grace of God."[2]

But although religious and political forces were powerful allies in loosening the web of hereditary privilege, it was the Industrial Revolution that forced the issue. Once its full impact was felt, societies of hereditary status could never again be quite the same. The only question was what would come next. We shall concern ourselves here with only one aspect of what came next, namely, the ways in which the new societies dealt with differences in individual ability and performance.

Most of those who fought to abolish social hierarchies saw the stratified society as the only significant factor that created differences in status between people, and they imagined that the removal of that factor would greatly diminish such differences—perhaps erase them altogether. But when individuals were released from the fetters on performance characteristic of a stratified society, great individual differences in performance emerged and led to peaks and valleys of status as dramatic as those produced by hereditary stratification. Many a feudal lord would have given his drawbridge to enjoy the power and glory of the industrial barons who pushed him into the history books.

When a society gives up hereditary stratification, there are two ways in which it may deal with the dramatic individual differences in ability and performance that emerge. One way is to limit or work against such individual differences, protecting the slow runners and curbing the swift. This, roughly speaking, is the path of equalitarianism. The other way is simply to let individual differences determine the result. As we shall see, in their moderate forms each of these points of view— equalitarianism and unfettered individual performance—is a necessary ingredient of a healthy society (as we conceive health in a society). We shall also see that each can be carried to harmful extremes.

Each position, in its more moderate form, represents a facet of the American ideal. *"Zwei Seelen wohnen, ach! in meiner Brust,"* Faust said. The "two souls" in the breast of most Americans are devotion to equality (with certain serious lapses we shall discuss later) and attachment to individual achievement. The possibility that the two views might often conflict doesn't occur to them. Their sentiments are those of the Irishman who cried, "I'm as good as you are, and a great deal better too!"

In their extreme forms the two positions are mutually exclusive. But very few societies have encouraged anything approaching extreme equalitarianism (certainly the Soviet Union has not); and very few have come close to an unbridled emphasis upon individual performance.

The Vitality of Nephewism

Americans dislike the principle of hereditary privilege, so they tend not to talk about it. But ignoring it does not make it go away. Only the nations most profoundly affected by the Industrial Revolution discarded the patterns of hereditary stratification. The majority of societies in the world, even today, show a considerable degree of stratification. In Africa today one may observe hereditary tribal leadership existing alongside newer forms of representative government in the same community. It is correct to say that the consequences are confusing.

But even in those countries that experienced the full impact of the Industrial Revolution, the old way of organizing society held on with surprising stubbornness.

Hereditary privilege has been relatively weak in the United States, which acquired its distinctive character at precisely the time in history when the old ways were under most vigorous attack and the new ways gaining their first foothold. The colonists left the old patterns behind them and found in America a *tabula rasa* on which to sketch the character of a new society. Much the same may be said of Australia, New Zealand, and Canada.

Yet even in the United States one finds unmistakable vestiges of a stratified society. The "old families" of Boston, Philadelphia, Baltimore, and Charleston may have grown a bit moldy, but they have survived. Vestiges of an earlier way of thinking about social class may be observed in the society columns of the newspapers, in the fashionable prep schools, in the exclusive clubs, and even in the casual conversations of many Americans.

The truth is that the characteristics of human interaction and social organization that produced societies of hereditary privilege in the first place have not changed. Indeed, the tendency is so deeply rooted in human interaction that if one could eliminate every trace of it today, it would begin to creep back tomorrow. Every parent is a potential dynast. (Ask any college admissions officer.)

This is not to say that the newer forms of social organization are ephemeral, nor that we should anticipate the return of aristocracies in the old pattern. It does mean that the older forms of social organization grew out of something enduring in the nature of human interaction and that, given appropriate circumstances, this "something enduring" could easily re-create at least some of the patterns we thought we had put behind us.

People find that there are many times in life when they are delighted to accept some good thing that comes to them not because they earned it, and not because it is their fair share of something everyone else received too, but simply because they stand in a family relationship to the donor, or occupy a certain position in the community, or are members of the same lodge as the donor. Similarly, almost everyone who makes decisions with respect to others—recruitment, promotions, job assignments, and the like—has occasionally based those decisions not strictly on performance or character or a fair sharing of favors but on the fact that the person involved was a relative, a friend, or a parishioner of the same church. This is a far cry from a society of hereditary status. But it is the seed from which such societies grow. Any favoritism that judges individuals on the basis of their relationships rather than on ability and character is a seed that, properly nourished, can eventually produce a full-blown society of hereditary status.

This is true of nepotism—literally *nephewism*—wherever it occurs: in business, in government, or in any other organization. When the grand old man who founded a corporation forty years ago moves up to the board chairmanship and places his son in the president's office, he is exhibiting in a contemporary setting the quite understandable human impulse that produced systems of hereditary status. The mayor of a Western city was recently under political attack for having placed no fewer than fourteen relatives in city jobs. The fraternity that gives special consideration to "legacies" (i.e., relatives of present members), the college that gives special consideration to children of alumni, the clubs that weigh family background in selecting new members, the mother who doesn't want her son to marry "below his station"—all are examples of the continuing vigor of the impulses that led originally to hereditary stratification.[3]

All of this is interesting but not alarming. The pressures

toward hereditary stratification are outweighed by far more powerful forces in American life.

Observers who are curious about such matters might find it interesting to keep a sharp eye on aristocracies of profession, which have rather impressive survival value in our present social structure. One is bound to note and reflect on the number of academic children of academic parents, military children of military parents, and so forth. Even in the second generation of such families one gains a strong impression of entrenched attitudes, of a sense of membership in a special world, and of a developing separation from the world at large.

At a reception following the commencement ceremony at one of our leading universities, a biologist whom I had known for years introduced me to his prospective son-in-law and confided later that he was disappointed in his daughter's choice. I asked about his objections to the lad (who had impressed me.) Was he stupid? No. Lazy? No. Ill-tempered? No. Finally my friend grinned wryly and said, "He works in a bank. He even wants to be president of it eventually."

"Is that bad?" I asked.

"Well, no . . . but I had hoped she'd pick a scientist—or at least an academic man. I don't even know how to talk to a banker!"

CHAPTER TWO

Individual Achievement versus Equality

A S WE HAVE SEEN, the demise of societies of hereditary stratification stirred two contradictory—at least partially contradictory—hopes: one was that was that everyone would be free to perform at the level of his or her ability, motivation, and qualities of character and be rewarded accordingly; the other was that all would be equal. (As we shall see in the chapter on civil rights, there were tragic exceptions to the American belief in equality, exceptions so momentous that they must be discussed in their own context.)

Individual Achievement

Many Americans have always assumed that the only sensible way to organize society is to allow individuals to enjoy whatever status, privileges, and power they are capable of winning for themselves in the general striving. The achievement might be a solo performance or it might be part of a team or cooperative activity; obviously much of what we speak of as individual achievement takes place in a team context.

In its more moderate forms, the emphasis upon individual achievement has been salutary. Historically no feature of our society has been more treasured than the opportunity for individuals to realize the promise that is in them and to achieve status in terms of their own performance. Frederick Jackson Turner wrote, "Western democracy through the whole of its earlier period tended to the production of a society of which the most distinctive fact was the freedom of the individual to rise under conditions of social mobility. . . ."[1]

These are values we would never willingly relinquish. Abraham Lincoln, born in a log cabin; Andrew Carnegie, the son of a poor Scottish weaver; Ezra Cornell, starting life as a carpenter and mill hand—these are favored snapshots in our national family album. In 1856, when a statue of Benjamin Franklin was unveiled in Boston, the principal speaker said, "Behold him, ye that are humblest and poorest in present condition or in future prospect,—lift up your heads and look at the image of a man who rose from nothing, who owed nothing to parentage . . . but who lived to stand before kings, . . ."[2]

Woodrow Wilson observed that democracy "releases the energies of every human being" and that this was one of the most significant consequences of the dissolution of stratified societies.

"No sooner do you set foot upon American ground, said de Tocqueville in 1835, "than you are stunned by a kind of tumult. Everything is in motion. . . . "[3] Said another observer, "A feverish activity seems to obsess these inhabitants of North America."[4] And Alistair Cooke said in 1952, "America may end in spontaneous combustion, but never in apathy, inertia or uninventiveness."[5]

Societies of hereditary privilege kept a lid on the aspirations of most individuals. With the lid removed, aspirations soared. People dared to hope, and they dared act in pursuit of their hopes. And constantly reinforcing their hope was the drama of "hidden gifts discovered." Few themes have gripped the imagination of Americans so intensely as the discovery of talent in unexpected places—the slum child who shows scientific genius, the frail youngster who develops athletic skills, the poor boy who becomes a captain of industry. Our popular literature and our folklore are filled with such images. They encourage self-discovery, stir ambition, and inspire emulation.

More objective evidence of our emphasis on individual performance is the impressive increase in the use of standardized aptitude and achievement tests. Neither a society of hereditary privilege nor a society of extreme equalitarianism would use such tests with enthusiasm. (I shall discuss in a later chapter some of the problems associated with the tests.)

But release from hereditary stratification brought problems as well as opportunities for individuals. Sometimes it gave them only the freedom to be crushed by the new forces of industrial society. And while it offered them freedom to achieve, it placed new burdens of responsibility and pressure on them. Among the consequences were not only exhilaration but anxiety, not only self-discovery but fear.

It soon became apparent that emphasis on individual performance can be pushed to extremes; and we now know that there are hazards in such extremes. "Everyone for himself and the devil take the hindmost" is a colorful saying but an unworkable model for social organization. No society has ever fully tested this manner of organizing human relationships—for the very good reason that any society which carried the principle to its logical conclusion would tear itself to pieces. The laws against mayhem and murder, for example, are designed to prevent ruthless members of society from enjoying the fruits of their ruthlessness.

But even within the bounds of the law, extreme emphasis on performance as a criterion of status may foster an atmosphere of raw striving that results in brutal treatment of the less able, or less vigorous, or less aggressive; it may wantonly injure those whose temperament or whose values make them unwilling to engage in performance rivalries; it may penalize those whose undeniable excellences do not add up to the kinds of performance that the society at any given moment chooses to reward; and it may victimize those who can't fight back, e.g., children.

Some of the casualties of such a system were paraded before the Ashley Mines Investigation Commission in England in 1842, among them Sarah Gooder. Here is Sarah's view of a world she never made:

I am Sarah Gooder, I am eight years old. I'm a coal carrier in the Gawber Mine. It does not tire me, but I have to trap without a light and I'm scared. I go at four and sometimes half past three in the morning, and come out at five and half past in the evening. I never go to sleep. Sometimes I sing when I've light, but not in the dark; I dare not sing then. I don't like being in the pit. I am very sleepy when I go in the morning. I go to Sunday school and learn to read. They teach me to pray. I have heard tell of Jesus many a time. I don't know why he came on earth. I don't know why he died, but he had stones for his head to rest on.[6]

But the brutalities of the early days of the Industrial Revolution were not the only sources of difficulty. There were other and more subtle hazards yet to come.

In a society of hereditary privilege, an individual of humble position might not have been wholly happy with his lot, but he had never had reason to look forward to any other fate. Never having had prospects of betterment, he could hardly be disillusioned. He entertained no hopes, but neither was he nagged by ambition. When the new democracies removed the ceiling on expectations, nothing could have been more satisfying for those with the energy, ability, and emotional balance to meet the challenge. But to the individual lacking in these qualities, the new system was fraught with danger. Lack of ability, lack of energy, or lack of aggressiveness led to frustration and failure. Sometimes obsessive ambition led to emotional breakdown. Unrealistic ambitions led to bitter defeats.

No system that issues an open invitation to every youngster to "shoot high" can avoid facing the fact that room at the top is limited. A study done in the 1950s reported that four-fifths of young people aspired to high-level jobs, of which there were only enough to occupy one-fifth of our labor force.[7] Such figures suggest a tremendous amount of human disappointment.

The United States has never committed itself to extreme emphasis upon individual performance, but at times it has come close.

Equality

During the California gold rush, Mrs. Clappe, a physician's wife living in one of the mining camps on the north fork of the Feather River, made the following entry in her journal:

September 4, 1852
    Last night one of our neighbors had a dinner party. He came in to borrow a teaspoon. "Had you not better take them all?" I said. "Oh, no," was the answer, "that would be too much luxury. My guests are not used to it, and they would think that I was getting aristocratic, and putting on airs. One is enough; they can pass it 'round from one to the other."[8]

It was from such frontier conditions that much of our equalitarianism sprang. Americans love the idea of equality (though as we shall see later they don't always love the fact of equality.)

But what is it that they love? The incident on the Feather River gives no clue to the enduring content of American equalitarianism. Our devotion to the one-spoon dining service has not proved durable. What does equality mean for Americans?

Anyone who sets out to comment on equality without the training of a professional philosopher is bound to be somewhat intimidated by the impressive and extended analyses of scholars such as Robert Nozick, John Rawls, and Michael Walzer —to mention only three.[9] But given the magisterial disagreement among them, perhaps there is room for venturesome nonphilosophers in the interstices.

It is possible to suggest the views that would probably receive general endorsement in this country today. First of all, we believe that in the final matters of life and death all humans are equally worthy of our care and concern. "We come equals into this world," said George Mason in 1775, "and equals shall we go out of it."[10] Chesterton meant something not very different when he reminded us that in an accident at sea we do not cry, "Bad citizen overboard!"[11]

Beyond this we believe that all are equal in the possession of certain legal, civil, and political rights. We believe with Aristotle that the only stable state is the one in which all are equal before the law.[12] Our Constitution is, among other things, a compendium of the rights we possess equally.

But we know that individuals are not equal in their native gifts nor their qualities of character nor their motivation; and it follows that they will not be equal in their achievements. That is why we give *equality of opportunity* such a central role in our social philosophy. "We may not all hit home runs," the saying goes, "but everyone should have a chance at bat." (In the debates of recent years, "equality of opportunity" hasn't turned out to be so simple a concept, and I shall explore it at greater depth in a later chapter.)

There have always been—since the eighteenth century— some Americans with a view of equalitarianism that can only be described as extreme. These Americans have always gone considerably beyond commonly held views, insisting that no one should be regarded as better than anyone else in any dimension and that there should be no difference whatever in status or income.

Equalitarians holding these extreme views have tended to believe that individuals of great leadership capacities, great energies, or greatly superior aptitudes are more trouble to society than they are worth. Lionel Trilling says, " . . . all the instincts or necessities of radical democracy are against the superbness and arbitrariness which often mark great spirits."[13] Merle Curti reminds us that in the Jacksonian era in this country equalitarianism reached such heights that trained personnel in the public service were considered unnecessary. "The democratic faith further held that no special group might make the difference between life and death."[14] Thus, in the West, even licensing of physicians was lax, because not to be lax was thought to be undemocratic!

This same impulse may be observed in some of our local political contests in which constituents favor the candidate who seems to be saying that he is not in any respect superior to the average voter, and perhaps a little inferior. "Friends, rednecks, suckers, and fellow hicks" was Willie Stark's greeting to the voters.[15]

The same attitudes are observable in the widespread social pressure to play down one's gifts. One of the requirements of social effectiveness in many segments of our national life is that one not arouse envy through an unseemly display of intelligence or talent. One must be, above all, unthreatening to the other fellow's self-esteem. In this atmosphere it will surprise no one to learn that deliberately slovenly speech, the studied fumble, and the calculated inelegance have achieved the status of minor art forms. And the phrase "I'm just a country boy" has become the favored gambit of sophisticated and wily men.

The ultimate consequence of movement in that direction is all too familiar to us: a rejection of all standards and tolerance of mediocrity and shabbiness in every aspect of our national life. We have seen mediocrity breed mediocrity. We now begin to understand what Kierkegaard meant when he warned us of the danger of an equalitarianism so extreme as to be "unrelieved by even the smallest eminence."[16]

We might as well admit that it is not easy for us as believers in democracy to dwell on the differences in capacity between individuals. Democratic philosophy has tended to ignore such differences where possible and to belittle them when it could not ignore them. And it has had some grounds for doing so: the enemies of democracy have often cited the unequal capacities of individuals as an excuse for institutions that violate our most deeply held beliefs. But extreme equalitarianism, or, as I would prefer to say, *equalitarianism wrongly conceived*—which ignores differences in native capacity and achievement and eliminates incentives to individual performance—has not served democracy well. Carried far enough, it means the end of that striving for excellence that has produced history's greatest achievements.

Although the United States has never chosen the path of extreme equalitarianism, the philosophy has many adherents— perhaps unwitting—in our midst. And this will not change.

CHAPTER THREE

The Three-Way Contest

NOTE THAT the three competing principles—hereditary privilege, equalitarianism, and rewards for individual performance—may all be present in the same society. The relative strength of the three principles may vary from one activity to another within the same community. There are, for example, American communities that are fairly stratified in the strictly social dimension of life, relatively equalitarian in education, and committed to individual performance in economic matters.

And to complicate the picture further, the three principles do not always function independently. For example, the adherents of any two of them may form an alliance to attack the third. The aristocrat and the thoroughgoing equalitarian can find common ground in their dislike of the successful self-made man and will sometimes combine against him. He returns the hostility, knowing that he could not have risen so easily in a purely aristocratic society or in an extremely equalitarian one.

At other times, the self-made individuals in a society may readily form an alliance with the aristocratic elements in order to combat equalitarian movements. Indeed, this alliance—of old families and new dollars—has been the foundation stone of American political conservatism.

Individuals of great ability and ambition are not apt to be strong proponents of equalitarianism. But here again we find alliances of convenience. The discovery by vigorous leaders that alliance with the masses could carry them to their objectives is as old as recorded history.

When David was in the Cave of Adullam, "everyone that was in distress, and everyone that was in debt, and everyone that was discontented, gathered themselves unto him; and he became a captain over them. . . . "[1]

In G. B. Shaw's *The Apple Cart,* the demagogue Boanerges describes his way of dealing with the people:

> I talk democracy to these men and women. I tell them that they have the vote, and that theirs is the kingdom; and the power and the glory. I say to them, "You are supreme: exercise your power." They say, "That's right: tell us what to do"; and I tell them. I say, "Exercise your vote intelligently by voting for me." And they do. That's democracy; and a splendid thing it is too for putting the right men in the right place.[2]

Worldwide, it has now become conventional for power-hungry leaders to ally themselves with the masses. Huey Long was a brilliant performer in the new phase of the ancient art. Juan Perón was another.

A curious anomaly is that under conditions of equalitarianism gifted individuals may even develop intensified drives for excellence. Harold Nicolson suggested that what he regarded as the depressing atmosphere of mediocrity in England in the 1950s may have been more stimulating to the occasional genius than would the presence of innumerable competing geniuses.[3] In this connection, it has always struck me as a matter of singular interest that Edmund Hillary came out of the flattest social landscape in the world and climbed the highest mountain in the world. Geographically New Zealand is all peaks and valleys, but socially it is a featureless plain. What that may have contributed to Sir Edmund's great performance is a matter for speculation.

Finally, extreme emphasis on rewards for individual performance may lead to mutually protective measures that nullify that emphasis. In an organization or society that places exclusive stress on individual performance there arise such searing rivalries, such pervading insecurity that cooperation is undermined and large numbers of individuals seek shelter from the chill wind of unmitigated competition.

Both union and business practices illustrate the point. It is sometimes said that while the ordinary mortal dreads excessive competition, the businessman loves it. But the record shows that businessmen can move very swiftly to protect themselves against the harsher manifestations of competition. Out of this impulse come price-fixing agreements, protectionist legislation, and innumerable other devices in restraint of trade.

Internal versus External Pressures

Extreme emphasis on individual performance produces consequences that are threatening to so many people within an organization (or society) that there arise powerful *internal* forces to combat the emphasis. On the other hand, in an organization or society characterized by extreme equalitarianism the greatest threat may lie in *external competition,* i.e., from aggressive organizations or societies that have not fettered their most talented and energetic people.

This holds an interesting lesson for us as a nation. To the extent that we move toward dangerous excesses of emphasis on rewards for individual performance, we can probably count on self-corrective forces from within our own society. To the extent that we move toward excesses of equalitarianism, we may learn our lesson only at the hands of more vigorous outsiders.

Bureaucracy

It remains to describe a contemporary form that is a curious combination of stratification and equalitarianism: the old-line, conventional bureaucracy. It is hierarchic but it is not the preordained stratification of class or caste. It has many strata and each stratum treasures the things that distinguish it from the strata below—and yet there may be a high degree of equalitarianism at any given level, e.g., a given grade level in the Civil Service. This is the kind of organization in which seniority weighs heavily in promotion, and the chief way to win points is to grow older. Much of the rough and tumble of competition has been eliminated.

It is not surprising, then, that modern corporate leaders seeking to release creativity in their workers find themselves combating the conventional bureaucratic forms that have dominated so many old-line corporations, for example, by reducing the number of strata, cutting the formality of communication up and down the line, and so on. In doing so, they are not functioning as equalitarians; they are seeking to release the possibilities of individual performance.

Unresolvable Tensions

No doubt a substantial emphasis on individual performance will continue to be a vital ingredient in our social functioning. An environment that provides freedom and incentives for the energetic action, the striving, the zeal and zest that are so often released in individual performance is conducive to excellence and creativity.

But it would be foolish to pretend that all the activity so produced is attractive. It may reflect a commitment to excellence, a drive to learn, explore, build, lead, be admired, express literary, artistic, or spiritual impulses; or it may reflect, less attractively, an obsessive desire to accumulate, wield power, conquer, and exploit.

In its moderate forms—and held within bounds—emphasis on individual achievement allows a healthy play of individual gifts, holds out an invitation to excel, but does not necessarily sanction the ruthless subordination of those who are less able, less vigorous, or less aggressive. In its extreme forms, emphasis on individual performance destroys cooperative endeavor and can lead to something close to the law of the jungle: let those who can, survive; let others go under. Few Americans are prepared to accept anything approaching that extreme.

Just as there will always be some individuals with powerful impulses to achieve and excel, so there will always emerge a variety of protective measures to shield others from the harsher consequences of individual comparison.

In its moderate forms, equalitarianism prohibits ruthlessness in the strong, protects the weak from wanton injury, and
defines certain areas of equality that must not be transgressed;
but it does not seek altogether to eliminate individual differences or their consequences. Moderate equalitarianism has produced innumerable measures that most enlightened Americans
regard as essential, from the Bill of Rights to minimum-wage
laws, from the graduated income tax to the principle that each
citizen has one vote—to mention only a few.

In its extreme forms, equalitarianism denies that there are
inequalities in capacity, eliminates situations in which such
inequalities might exhibit themselves, and insures that if such
differences do emerge, they will not result in differences in
status.

In the light of these considerations, one may see how ar-
chaic are analyses which treat such matters in terms of the
labels "Jacksonianism," "Jeffersonianism," and so forth, or
which assume that any position taken with respect to individual differences may be characterized as either "pro-elite" or
"pro-masses," as "aristocratic" or "democratic." Such primitive categories serve only to mask reality.

If our society is to hold in balance the contesting impulses
we have been discussing, citizens must understand the implications of each. We have never been willing to explore those
implications candidly and incisively.

CHAPTER FOUR

Civil Rights

The Struggle for Racial Justice

AT SOME RISK TO the completeness of the preceding chapters I have postponed discussion of a circumstance that must affect profoundly any discussion of equality in the United States. That circumstance is that there continued into mid-twentieth-century America a grotesquely anachronistic caste system for black Americans. For Negroes, ours was a society of hereditary stratification from colonial days.

I ask the reader to bear with me in a brief review of the struggle against that anachronism. Most of it will be familiar to adult readers, but some of it is a necessary prelude to discussion of the complex issues that have arisen.

To understand the tendency of blacks to be profoundly

depressed by any loss of momentum in the struggle, one must first understand that the story is characterized by long periods of inaction. In 1776 we proclaimed to the world that "all men are created equal." Eighty-seven years elapsed before Lincoln issued his Emancipation Proclamation. That's a long time to wait.

We fought a tragic and bloody war to free the slaves, and their rights as free citizens were embedded in the Thirteenth, Fourteenth, and Fifteenth amendments to the Constitution. After the Civil War, Congress passed rudimentary civil rights legislation, but the Supreme Court invalidated much of it, and it left no mark whatever after the period of Reconstruction. Worse yet, the Court chose to interpret the post-Civil War amendments in such a way as to minimize their impact on civil rights. More than three-quarters of a century passed before the Court faced up to the post-Civil War amendments. That's a long time too.

In 1896 the Court, still in its prosegregation phase, laid down its "separate but equal" doctrine in Plessy v. Ferguson, and only Justice Harlan (whose grandson was to serve on the Court sixty years later) disagreed—in his famous "Our Constitution is color-blind" dissent.

At the end of the century, white supremacy was unchallenged and there were scores of lynchings each year. Throughout the South, state and local laws segregated the races in schools, hospitals, hotels, restaurants, conveyances, and places of recreation. Intermarriage was forbidden. Negroes could not vote and could not serve on juries. Discrimination pervaded the society.

In the first half of the twentieth century there were events foreshadowing major change, e.g., founding of the National Association for the Advancement of Colored People in 1910, shrewd and successful litigation by that organization in the thirties and forties, and President Roosevelt's banning of discrimination in defense industries (1941). President Truman ended segregation in the armed forces, banned discrimination in federal employment, and made civil rights such an issue of his administration that a portion of the Democratic Party, calling themselves "Dixiecrats," broke away and ran Senator Strom Thurmond as their candidate for president.

But the climactic years were yet to come. In the 1950s and 1960s events occurred that future historians will be writing about long after most crises of the mid-twentieth century are forgotten.

In 1952 and 1953 the NAACP Legal Defense and Educational Fund argued in a series of lawsuits that school segregation in Delaware, the District of Columbia, Kansas, South Carolina, and Virginia should be ruled unconstitutional. The cases, grouped under the name of the Topeka, Kansas, suit—*Brown* v. *Board of Education*—achieved their place in history on May 17, 1954, when the Supreme Court, acting unanimously, set aside the "separate but equal" doctrine and forbade the states to impose racial segregation in the public schools. "Separate educational facilities," the Court ruled, "are inherently unequal."

It was a stunning event. Kierkegaard once said, "Most people really believe that the Christian commandments (e.g., to love one's neighbor as oneself) are intentionally a little too severe—like putting the clock ahead half an hour to make sure of not being late in the morning."

A good many Americans had come to think of the Constitution in just those terms as it applied to the rights of black Americans. The Brown decision was a simple assertion that the Constitution meant what it said. Not surprisingly, the pace of events in the civil rights struggle quickened. That Southern leaders chose to pursue a course of "massive resistance" simply heightened the liveliness of the conflict.

In 1955, in Montgomery, Alabama, Rosa Parks was arrested for refusing to give up her seat to a white man in a crowded bus—touching off the boycott that first brought the Reverend Martin Luther King, Jr., to national attention. With that event, the civil rights struggle emerged from its era of quiet litigation and became a public movement.

In 1957 the first Civil Rights Act since Reconstruction was passed by Congress; and that same year President Eisenhower, facing the intention of Governor Faubus to defy school desegregation decisions of federal courts, federalized the Arkansas National Guard and sent the 101st Airborne Division to Little Rock.

In 1960 four black college freshmen staged a sit-in in Greensboro, South Carolina, at a lunch counter where they had been refused service. That same year the Student Nonviolent Coordinating Committee was formed. For two years the tempo of activity increased steadily, climaxing in the events of 1963: television viewers throughout America saw the Birmingham police using cattle prods, firehoses, and police dogs against nonviolent civil rights demonstrators; President Kennedy intervened to uphold a court order to desegregate the University of Alabama; Medgar Evers, an NAACP field organizer in Mississippi, was murdered; four black children were killed in a church bombing in Birmingham; and the Reverend King led his historic March on Washington.

Following President Kennedy's assassination in November of that fateful year, President Johnson set out to pass new civil rights legislation. On July 2, 1964, he signed the Civil Rights Act of 1964. It remained to enforce that extraordinary piece of legislation.

The assassinations of President Kennedy, Robert F. Kennedy, and Martin Luther King, Jr., the bitter domestic conflict over Vietnam, urban riots of unprecedented magnitude, and finally the wrenching scandal of Watergate made the period from November 1963 to August 1974 a nightmare decade for the American people. No one who shared in the events of that period will ever forget them.

Statistics cannot reflect the emotional intensity of the civil rights effort, but in this brief recounting, numbers will have to do.

Progress in school desegregation in the first eleven years following the Brown decision had been very modest indeed. But when the federal government made it known that it would enforce the Civil Rights Act by withholding funds available to school districts under the 1965 Elementary and Secondary Education Act unless progress was made, desegregation began in earnest. In 1964 roughly 2 percent of the South's black students attended schools with whites. By 1968 it was 32 percent; by 1978 it was 91 percent.

At the college level black enrollment tripled during the 1960s (from 174,000 to 522,000). Then from 1970 to 1976 it doubled to more than one million.

The consequences of centuries of discrimination aren't ended in a day, but by any standard, the two decades beginning in 1954 were historic.

Though the story centered around blacks, it was also of importance to American Indians and to Mexican Americans; and in fact the latter groups benefited importantly by lessons learned in the earlier struggle.

The story of women's struggle to gain recognition of their civil rights overlaps but is sufficiently different to deserve separate comment. The first great wave of the women's movement started with the suffragists in the nineteenth century and cul-

minated in the Nineteenth Amendment (1920). The second
wave gathered force in the 1960s and 1970s and is still going
strong. The women's movement may be, in the long perspective of history, more epoch-making than the fight for racial
justice. With the rarest exceptions, women have been subjugated by civilizations of every race and skin color. Their emergence into the light is an event of extraordinary significance
and—compared to the racial struggle—may ultimately have
more far-reaching consequences for human social organization.

Despite the occasionally gloomy views of minority and
women's leaders, neither of these movements can ever be re-
versed. Aspirations and expectations have been released that
can never be put back in the box.

Civil Rights Issues

But the striking victories of the 1960s and 1970s left a
legacy of thorny issues.

Up through 1964 the goals of the civil rights movement
were clear and uncomplicated: to bring about, through litigation, legislation, and public protest, a condition in which any
individual black could have access on equal terms to the institutions and opportunities of white society. The society was to be
"color-blind."

And, ironically, by 1964 many Southern leaders would have
been glad to settle for the "color blindness" that had seemed
so offensive when the first Justice Harlan espoused it seventy
years earlier. They feared that civil rights leaders would go
beyond the relative neutrality of color blindness to an aggressive pursuit of racial balance. And of course that is precisely
what happened.

First of all, in order for government leaders to know whether school officials and recruiting officers were actually desegregating, they sought measurable reductions in racial separateness. That meant counting, and it meant taking account of color.

Second, Judge John Minor Wisdom of the Fifth Circuit Court of Appeals, building on earlier decisions, ruled that in districts where *de jure* segregation had existed integration was the goal—not merely desegregation.

It was a striking shift: from color blindness to color consciousness, from desegregation to integration, from individual rights to a concept of group representation. It led inevitably to busing to achieve racial balance. And it led to affirmative action.

Of all civil rights policies, the most controversial was busing. Opinion polls showed a consistent and substantial opposition to it. Dispassionate observation revealed that when judiciously used it could achieve good results, but that less judiciously used it could produce bad results. One of the bad results was white flight to the suburbs, a consequence that none of the friends of civil rights found it very easy to think about or deal with. Black leaders themselves were of two minds on the subject of busing. All had welcomed the policy as a means of achieving racial balance, but in time many concluded that, under some circumstances, they preferred the strengthening of their own neighborhood schools rather than a city-wide busing system.

Affirmative action traveled a road only slightly less rocky. It was first formulated in an executive order issued by President Johnson in 1965 (amended in 1967). Employers were actively to seek out minority group applicants, provide special training where necessary, and hire preferentially to correct underrepresentation of minority groups. Affirmative action does not lead inevitably to quotas, but quotas (in one form or another) were a common result.

Universities were particularly concerned by the new turn of events because they feared that the principle of proportional group representation would replace the criterion of merit in selection of graduate students and faculty. They feared the emergence of a double standard for admissions and "second-class citizenship" for the blacks admitted under such a standard. And they wondered where the principle of group representation would carry them as it went beyond black Americans. Would all ethnic groups require similar treatment?

But the issue that precipitated the definitive Supreme Court ruling on the subject was reverse discrimination. Alan Bakke, a white applicant who had not been accepted by the medical school of the University of California at Davis, brought the suit. The school had a dual admissions system: in addition to the eighty-four places for which whites could compete, there were sixteen places for which only minority group applicants could compete. Bakke's scores on the Medical College Admissions tests were considerably above the average of those admitted in the minority category, and the Supreme Court ruled in 1978 that he had been the victim of "explicit racial classification."

The Court did not say that it was wrong to take race into account; it did not rule out affirmative action broadly conceived. The Court did, however, rule against the use of a "specific percentage"—in other words, quotas.

Another set of issues had come to the surface earlier as the result of a highly controversial study issued by James S. Coleman in 1966.[1] Briefly, Coleman concluded that the schools attended by black students—contrary to popular opinion—

were not markedly inferior to those attended by white students; that achievement was much more heavily determined by family background than by the quality of the school; and that black children seemed to do better in majority white schools.

The intense debate over the validity of the Coleman findings did not diminish the impact of the study. To a considerable fraction of civil rights leadership it seemed to say that the immense effort being made toward "compensatory education" for disadvantaged blacks was beside the point (since school programs as such were not—according to the study— the main factor in unequal achievement). And second, it seemed to say that the answer was at all costs to disperse black children into white schools. The U.S. Civil Rights Commission, in its 1967 report entitled *Racial Isolation,* picked up the themes. It spoke critically of compensatory education and strongly urged dispersion.

Social scientists disagree sharply among themselves concerning the Coleman findings. Later studies did not confirm his finding that black students educated in majority white schools attained more or had greater self-esteem. And then Coleman himself issued a new study in 1975 asserting that court-imposed desegregation was contributing to white flight to the suburbs.

In short, the civil rights movement became caught in a tangle of issues that were controversial even within the movement itself. How these issues eventually sort themselves out will depend on future court decisions, demographic changes, and many other factors, not least—one may hope—a stabilization of social science findings on the relevant issues.

But the issues and arguments could not obscure the fact that the movement had produced consequences of historic magnitude.

CHAPTER FIVE

Equality of Opportunity or Result

T HE PHRASE "Equality of opportunity" is and will probably continue to be the expression most favored by
Americans to reflect their beliefs with respect to that
dimension of equality that has to do with achievement.

This is not to say that most Americans have thought very
hard about what equality of opportunity requires. It requires
the removal of every removable obstacle to the fulfillment of
the individual, whether prejudice, or ignorance, or treatable
physical impairment—whatever. It means that those without
status or wealth or membership in a privileged group will have
full access to opportunity.

We are far from having achieved equality of opportunity. In a society in which there are great differences in wealth, power, and status, free schooling may never compensate for the tremendous variations in opportunity represented by home background. When a New York social worker asked a Puerto Rican youngster whether there were any books in his home, the boy nodded proudly. "The telephone book," he explained. We cannot rest easy in the face of such inequality We must come as close as possible to making it a reality, and that requires positive, often extensive efforts. For the youngster just mentioned, the passage of a law declaring that there shall be no discrimination against him isn't enough. Steps must be taken to remedy the disadvantage with which he starts.

To say that there remain gross correctible inequalities of opportunity is not an attack on the principle itself. It just says that we haven't worked hard enough to live by the principle.

There's another caution to be expressed about the concept of equality of opportunity. In practice it means an equal chance to compete within the framework of goals and the structure of rules established by our particular society; and this tends to favor certain kinds of gifts. The society may insure my child equality of opportunity with every other child. But it can only place before him (and before all other children) the range of opportunities available in this particular society. If his undiscovered talent is for chariot racing or if he has the capacity to see visions, he may have missed his century. He may have any number of interesting or admirable qualities that this society doesn't choose to reward. This is unavoidable; but it is only proper to recognize that even if a society achieves perfect equality of opportunity, it will still inevitably favor some gifts over others.

Beginning in the 1960s a small but influential body of critics called into question the ideal of equal opportunity as the keystone of our thinking about equality. I do not share their views but I shall try to state their position fairly. The criticisms usually included one or more of the following lines of reasoning.

1) It was argued that inequalities of opportunity will *always* exist and that we are deceiving ourselves in our attempts to erase them.

2) It was charged that those who espouse equality of opportunity content themselves with the hope that everyone can be brought fairly to the starting line, and then they wash their hands of the destructive competitiveness that follows in which some reap fantastic rewards while others starve.

3) It was asserted that even if we could achieve equality of opportunity it would simply open the way to new inequalities of outcome based on the accidents of talent—which are no more fair, so the argument goes, than inequalities based on aristocratic family names. It isn't even fair to base differential rewards on qualities of character, according to this school of thought, since those are also allegedly based on the accident of good family background. As John Rawls put it, "Even the willingness to make an effort, to try, and so to be deserving in the ordinary sense, it itself dependent upon happy family and social circumstances."[1]

Those who shared these concerns concluded that we must devise arrangements that move toward *equality of results.* According to Rawls: "No one deserves his natural capacity, nor merits a more favorable starting place in society. . . . But . . . the basic structure can be arranged so that these contingencies work for the good of the least fortunate."[2]

And Christopher Jencks wrote:

Instead of trying to reduce people's capacity to gain a competitive advantage over one another we will have to change the rules of the game so as to reduce the rewards of competitive success and the costs of failure. Instead of trying to make everybody equally lucky or good at his job, we will have to devise "insurance" systems which neutralize the effects of luck, and income sharing systems which break the link between vocational success and living standards.[3]

But most students of the subject see real difficulties in proposing equality of results as a goal of social policy.

Those who believe in equality of results have focused their vision on differences in performance that stem from the unfair chances of life. Some people perform well because of genetic or cultural advantage. Is it fair to reward them differentially for performances that are in this sense "predetermined"? But the proponents of equality of results are so concerned about such "predetermined" outcomes that they ignore differential performances that most people regard as eminently worthy of praise or blame, performances reflecting sustained effort, character, and loyalty, on the one hand, or laziness and irresponsibility on the other. Most Americans are simply not ready for a world in which all behavior, worthy or unworthy, is conceived to be simply the accidental outcome of a genetic or cultural lottery and therefore not to be differentially rewarded.

Another commonly mentioned objection to the equality-of-results approach is that it takes no account of the role of incentives. The USSR, Yugoslavia, and most recently China have moved back toward incentives as a means of ensuring that the essential work of the society is carried on.

The other problem, pointed out by both philosophers and economists, is that the farther one goes in seeking equality of result, the more one must resort to government intervention.

The American people, if one may judge by studies of public opinion, take a rather balanced view of the issue. As indicated earlier, they have difficulty in accepting the equality-of-results approach. At the same time, it is clear that they do not want the principle of unrestrained competitive performance to govern unchallenged. They favor the progressive income tax and other measures to limit the extreme upper reaches of reward. And whatever corporate executives may tell themselves about the justifiability of astronomical salaries and unlimited perquisites, the public is not pleased.

At the other end of the scale, very few people would say: "Equality of opportunity is enough. Provide that, and then forget the losers." People generally believe that there is a point below which losers should not fall. As one writer pointed out, even if the gladiatorial contest were totally fair, we couldn't accept the practice of feeding the loser to the lions. Year after year, through liberal or conservative administrations, public opinion as measured by polls has shown strong support for social programs that care for the needy.

To sum up, the public generally accepts fairly wide discrepancies in reward but is opposed to excess at either end of the scale. It wants—in some measure—to curb excessive reward and to remedy excessive misery.

CHAPTER SIX

The Great Talent Hunt

The Demand for Educated Talent

I N THE LAST HALF OF the twentieth century there was not only a high level of concern for issues of equality but a greatly heightened awareness of the nation's need for educated talent.

William James foresaw the need much earlier. Speaking on the campus of Stanford University in 1906, he said, "The world . . . is only beginning to see that the wealth of a nation consists more than in anything else in the number of superior men that it harbors."[1]

James was generous in suggesting that the world shared his own prophetic understanding. Actually, he was half a century ahead of his time.

The fact is that we have witnessed a revolution in society's attitude toward men and women of high ability and advanced training. For the first time in history, such men and women are very much in demand. Throughout the ages, human societies have always been extravagantly wasteful of talent. Today, as a result of far-reaching social and technological developments, we are forced to search for talent and to use it effectively. Among the historic changes that have marked our era, this may in the long run prove to be one of the most profound.

After the USSR shattered our complacent sense of technological superiority by putting into orbit the first space satellite, *Sputnik*, in 1957, the question of whether we were properly nurturing talent became something of an obsession.

And the obsession again gripped us in the 1980s when Japanese industrial competition forced us to reexamine our educational practices. The overheated reaction to these two episodes has led some observers to suppose that the intense concern for trained talent is a fairly superficial, fear-driven phenomenon. It is not.

The demand for talent is an inevitable consequence of our stage of development as a society. As such, it has been rising for a long time. It is not a recent trend. We can observe societies in the world today at every stage of development from the most primitive to the most advanced, and nothing is easier to demonstrate than that every step toward the latter involves a heavier demand for educated talent. As Alfred North Whitehead put it, "In the conditions of modern life the rule is absolute, the race which does not value trained intelligence is doomed."[2]

The increasing demand for educated talent is firmly rooted in the level of technological complexity that is so characteristic of modern life, and in the complexity of present-day social organization. Even more important is the *rate of* change in both technological and social spheres. In a world that is rocking with change we need more than anything else a high capacity for adjustment to new circumstances, a capacity for innovation. The solutions we hit on today will be outmoded tomorrow. ("If it works, it's obsolete" is the witticism in fast-moving high technology companies.) Only ability and sound education equip one for the continuous seeking of new solutions. We don't even know what skills may be needed in the years ahead. That is why we must train our ablest young men and women in the fundamental fields of knowledge rather than the hot specialist fields of the moment, and must equip them to understand and cope with change. That is why we must give them the critical qualities of mind and the durable qualities of character that will serve them in circumstances we cannot now even predict.

It is not just technical competence that is needed. A society such as ours is dependent on many kinds of achievement, many kinds of complex understanding, many people with depth of judgment and perspective concerning the problems facing our world.

The importance of education is not limited to the higher orders of talent. A complex society is dependent every hour of every day upon the capacity of its people at every level to read and write, to make difficult judgments, and to act in the light of extensive information. The manager of a chemical plant said to me recently, "We can't even have an errand boy who isn't literate. Everything in this plant has to be handled with care." When there isn't a many-leveled base of trained talent on which to build, modern social and economic developments are simply impossible. And if that base were to disappear suddenly in any complex society, the whole intricate interlocking mechanism would grind to a halt.

The chief means of carrying on the talent hunt is the

educational system. Schools not only educate youngsters—they sort them out according to levels of ability. When the need for talent is great, the sifting tends to become rigorous.

There was a time—a fairly recent time—when education was *not* a rigorous sorting-out process. The demand for individuals of ability is now so familiar to us as to seem wholly unremarkable, but it constitutes a profound change in human affairs. Throughout the millennia of history, it has been the normal experience of mankind that only a few of the gifted individuals in a population have had the chance to develop their gifts. Generally speaking, individuals whose gifts have been discovered and cultivated have been as chance outcroppings of precious rock, while the great reserves of human talent lay undiscovered below.

In 1900 only about 4 percent of the college-age population went to college. For every youngster who went on with schooling, there were many just as bright who did not. The boy or girl without an education could look around and see plenty of able and ambitious young people in the same condition. Large numbers of children grew up in areas where schools were poor or nonexistent. Many energetic youngsters broke off schooling to pull their weight on the family farm or go west.

Most Americans approved of such decisions. The Horatio Alger heroes rarely held advanced academic degrees. In every machine shop and executive suite at the turn of the century, stories were swapped about the kid who went to college, learned a lot of fancy theory, and then made a mess of his first job.

Lord Palmerston, the British statesman, once said of Cornelius Vanderbilt that it was a pity a man of his ability had not had the advantage of formal schooling. When a friend passed this on to Vanderbilt, the latter snapped, "You tell Lord Palmerston from me that if I had learned education I would not have had time to learn anything else."[3]

At the turn of the century it was assumed that the only fields that required advanced training were medicine, law, the ministry, and the scholarly fields; and even in those fields the requirements were exceedingly flexible. Only a tiny proportion of leaders in other fields could boast college degrees.

Despite the foresight of men such as William James, the critical importance of human resources in modern society did not force itself to public attention until the latter half of the twentieth century, when the nation began to experience shortages in various professional and technical fields requiring advanced training, such as medicine, teaching, engineering, and physics.

As each profession faced shortages, each laid cool and aggressive plans to capture a bigger share of the oncoming stream of talent. Then it became apparent that the total stream was limited, and efforts to bring about the early identification, selection, and training of talented youngsters were intensified.

As a result, today's students face problems of which their great-grandfathers never dreamed. They know that their aptitudes and performance are being measured and predicted from the earliest grades of school. Every day's performance contributes to the inexorable summation that will decide their fate. They see the youngsters with the highest scores and grades move on to the most desirable colleges. They see industry's recruiters on the college campus asking for the highest-ranking students. They see the same youngsters heading off into the best jobs. Don't try to tell them how tough it was in the old days. Grandpa had it easy. A young mother, observing the strain on the bright youngsters and the pain of the less bright in the breakneck race for the finest colleges, said, "We're killing the best and giving up on the rest." Her assessment wasn't wholly accurate, but she recognized stress when she saw it.

Vestiges of Stratification

One of the obstacles to the full development of talent in our society is that we still have not learned to make the most of bright youngsters who begin life in impoverished surroundings.

In stratified societies, the amount of education received by a child depended upon his status in the society. If he was born to rank and wealth he had access to a good education. If he was born in the lower strata he usually did not. The educational system confirmed and held in place differences in status that were hereditarily determined. Thus was the class war, as well as other wars, won on the playing fields of Eton.

The history of American education has been one long campaign to get as far away from that kind of system as effort and ingenuity could take us. "Geniuses will be raked from the rubbish . . .," wrote Thomas Jefferson.[4]

But despite our system of public schools, poverty can still be a profound handicap and wealth a clear advantage. Families at the lowest economic level must all too often live in slum or near-slum areas where the schools do not attract the best teachers. Prosperous citizens can afford to live in expensive suburbs where the schools are sociologically not unlike the good independent prep schools.

But Coleman,[5] Jencks,[6] and others are no doubt right that for disadvantaged children the home can be a graver handicap than the school. Some of the problems associated with home background are well illustrated in a case brought to my attention some years ago. When Tom B. was a senior in high school, the principal told him his grades were high enough to get him to a good college. Tom took a job in an aircraft factory instead. The principal couldn't understand it, but most of Tom's family and friends would not have understood any other decision. Tom's father, an invalid whose own education ended with the fourth grade, was genuinely—if profanely—proud of Tom's attainments ("The kid talks like a——dictionary!") but thought the boy was already overeducated. His mother, a clerk in the five-and-ten, liked the idea of his going to college but needed his help to support the family. The wages offered by the factory looked like a fortune to Tom. He had worked part time since he was eight, but this was a man's job for a man's pay. He took it.

If he had had a fierce determination to go on to college, he might have found a way. But his diet was deficient in other things besides money. There were virtually no books in Tom's home. No one ever talked about ideas. No one ever mentioned educational goals. Most of Tom's friends in the run-down part of town where he lived had quit school long since. He had never had an informal out-of-school chat with anyone who reminisced about his own college years or recommended college to him. It is not surprising, then, that he had no awareness of what college could mean, no motivation to use his good mind, no aspirations that involved intellectual performance. The image of a fat paycheck from the aircraft company was very real; and the image of college was very dim.

Only in recent years have we come to the realization that these deficiencies are as damaging as any monetary handicap. The son of the city's leading lawyer had financial resources that Tom did not have; but even more important, he had an awareness of intellectual values and educational goals.

But it would be wrong to leave the impression that no progress has been made in the fight for educational opportunity. Marked inequalities still exist, but the great drama of American education has been the democratization of educational opportunity over the past century. It has been one of the great social revolutions. In emphasizing that much ground remains to be won, we must not belittle victories already achieved.

The Market for Talent

We have said that talent is very much in demand in our own society today. It is not true in all societies. And even in our own society not all kinds of talent are in demand at any one time.

An earnest young student from a South Asian country said to me, "You talk of the need for education in underdeveloped societies, but my problem is to find a job when I get back. Half my friends are unemployed intellectuals."

His problem is not unique. Part of the difficulty is that his country does not have the broad base of education at lower levels that makes a modern society possible. The young people they send abroad receive first-class modern educations and come back to a society that is not prepared to use their talents.

Another difficulty is that the fields in which these young people are educated are often chosen without regard to the needs of the society. In some Latin American countries, for example, large numbers of young people study law, even though the last thing their country may need is another lawyer. (Some of my friends would say the same of this country.)

Another problem is the view taken by some educated persons in these countries that their education entitles them to a job at a certain level of prestige. Instead of putting their superior knowledge to work on whatever tasks the society requires, they apply a social status test to job opportunities.

Even in our own society there may be overproduction of educated talent in specific lines. Indeed, on many occasions in the future there will be an imbalance between the number of individuals trained for a given line of work and the number of jobs available. Attempts will be made to minimize this through accurate forecasts of manpower needs, but experience with such forecasts has been discouraging. The alternative—and the wiser course—is to educate men and women who are capable of applying excellent fundamental training to a wide range of specific jobs.

The future will inevitably be hazardous for individuals who train themselves to do highly specific jobs and believe that society owes them a living in those lines of work. If technological change reduces demand for their specialty, they have nowhere to go. Had they been broadly trained in fundamental principles and willing to apply those principles in varying contexts over the years, they might have survived the ups and downs of the job market.

Of course, no society will ever provide a living for every kind of talent. We need not dwell on the fact that some kinds of talent—for picking pockets, let us say—have to be discouraged, nor that other kinds—the capacity to imitate bird calls, for example—are trivial. Even in the case of genuinely important gifts—the gifts of the artist, writer, composer, architect, or sculptor—the individual can never assume that society will support him in the exercise of his talent. Talent is one thing and the marketability of talent is something else. The latter will depend upon the kind and degree of talent involved, questions of supply and demand, the prosperity of the society, and many other things. It will never be easy for gifted individuals who are ahead of their time (or behind the times) or who exercise their talent in a way that does not coincide with the fashion of the moment.

Young people should not be misled in these matters. They must not be led to assume that there is always a market for talent. But while the individual must be realistic, teachers, curators, deans, critics, art dealers, editors, foundation officers, publishers—in short, all who are in a position to encourage talent—should continuously ask themselves whether the society is providing sufficient opportunities for its varied resources of talent. If important kinds of talent are withering on the vine, we had better know why.

CHAPTER SEVEN

The Identification of Talent

MY BOY IS something of a genius," said the commuter to his seat companion on the 5:26 P.M. train. He wasn't speaking metaphorically, he wasn't joking, and he wasn't consciously boasting. He said it in a matter-of-fact way, as he might have said, "My boy has a pet hamster." After pausing long enough to let his companion express a decent interest, he went on to report the basis for his judgment —the very high scores his youngster had made on a scholastic aptitude test.

Geniuses used to be rare. Today, thanks to popular interpretation of test scores, every elementary or secondary school has its quota.

The chief instrument used in the search for talent is the

standardized test. It would be surprising if the tests were not the object of considerable hostility.

Many fear that the tests will be inaccurate—that they will come up with an appraisal of Johnny that isn't fair to Johnny's talents. The fact that the tests may have high statistical reliability and validity does not quiet the apprehension. A neighbor of mine said, "They tell me the tests are right ninety-five percent of the time, but suppose my Billy is in the remaining five percent?"

Apprehension is heightened by the fact that it is very hard for those without professional training in psychology to understand the processes of mental measurement. No one wishes to be judged by a process he cannot comprehend.

Also, the tests bring vividly to mind the hazards of a society that engages in the large-scale processing of individuals. The neighbor quoted earlier put it this way: "I just resist the idea that my boy's life can be changed by a mark made electronically on a slip of paper a thousand miles away by an anonymous person or machine, acting on criteria unknown to me, and using a measuring instrument I can't comprehend." In short, there is not only fear of the tests but fear of the unknown bureaucracy that handles the testing and acts on the results.

No one concerned with the future of testing can affort to ignore these sources of anxiety. On the other hand, even if these sources of concern were to disappear, the hostility toward the tests would probably remain. The tests are designed to do an unpopular job. As the tests improve and become less vulnerable to present criticism, the hostility to them may actually increase. A proverbial phrase indicating complete rejection is "I wouldn't like it even if it were good." With tests, the more appropriate phrase might be "I wouldn't like them *especially* if they were good."

As a matter of fact some of the tests are excellent even today—*within the limits for which they were designed.* The development of standardized tests is one of the great success stories in the objective study of human behavior. Anyone who understands the problems of mental measurement must be impressed with the technical achievement these instruments represent.

It is now argued that the tests give an advantage to the individual of good family background and place the individual of poor family background at a disadvantage. This is true in some measure. But it must never be forgotten that the tests introduced an objectivity into the measurement of human abilities that never before existed. Before the tests were developed a great many people seriously believed that the less-educated segments of society were not *capable* of being educated. And the view is still prevalent in many societies.

An acquaintance of mine who recently visited a provincial school in France, where no objective tests were used, wrote: "The teacher seemed to find it impossible to separate his judgment of a pupil's intelligence from his judgment of the pupil's cleanliness, good manners, neatness of dress, and precision of speech. Needless to say, his students from the upper and upper middle social classes excelled in these qualities." Before the rise of objective tests American teachers were susceptible—at least in some degree—to the same social distortion of judgment. Against this background modern methods of mental measurement hit the educational system like a fresh breeze. The tests couldn't see whether the youngster was in rags or in tweeds, and they couldn't hear the accents of the slum. The tests revealed intellectual gifts at every level of the population.

This is not to say that the tests completely eliminate unfair advantage for the young person of privileged social back ground. They do not; and there must be continued efforts to improve the tests in that respect. But even with their imperfections they are in important respects more fair than methods previously used.

So anyone attacking the usefulness of the tests must suggest workable alternatives. It has been proved over and over again that the alternative methods of evaluating ability or achievement are also subject to errors and capable of doing injustice to those being judged. The best of the standardized tests have proven themselves to be dependable aids to judgment *when they are used cautiously and appropriately.* They are undeniably useful, undeniably limited instruments.

Let us examine the limitations. The best of the tests are on the whole quite effective in sorting out students according to their actual and potential performance in the classroom. But even in this context they are not perfect, and any school system that assumes them to be perfect will commit grave mistakes.

Of all mistakes made in using aptitude tests, perhaps the worst are made in trying to apply the results beyond the strictly academic or intellectual performances for which the tests were designed. Such mistakes occur for understandable reasons. Everyone knows that there are other powerful ingredients in successful performance—attitudes, values, motives, nonacademic talents—but it's very hard to measure those other ingredients. The temptation is almost overwhelming to lean too heavily on the effective—but limited—measures we do possess.

This error produces grievous difficulties when we try to identify young people who will exhibit high performance in later life. Performance in later life places rather heavy emphasis on precisely those attributes not measured by scholastic aptitude and achievement tests—zeal, character, judgment, staying power, and so on. Many years ago a talented youngster named Rennie D. was brought to my attention by his fond mother. Rennie was a gifted child of the most readily identifiable sort. He was extremely articulate, extremely quick in schoolwork. He was also lazy, self-indulgent, flaccid, and infantile in his emotions and personality, but these didn't interfere with his school performance. He was good-looking in a clean, open, pudgy way, and teachers loved him not only for his brightness but for his amiability. He sailed through school and college and graduated *magna cum laude,* as his mother assured me he would. But in the years since then he hasn't done a blessed thing.

We like to say that this is puzzling, but in fact it is not. Scholastic aptitude is a central ingredient in school performance and Rennie had it to a high degree. But there are other crucial ingredients in adult performance and he lacked them. Rennie is a vivid reminder that the tests were not designed to test success in life.

Wise Use of the Tests

We now know enough about the tests to suggest rules for minimizing the hazards and maximizing the benefits of these instruments.

By all odds the most important rule is that the tests should not be the sole reliance in identifying talent. Judgments of the youngster's scholastic aptitudes and achievements should be based on many kinds of evidence. The tests are one kind of evidence. School grades are another kind. The teachers' written judgments of the student are still another kind. The judgments of deans, principals, and counselors who have had dealings with the child may be useful. The important thing to be borne in mind is that every known measure of aptitudes and achievements has some failings. Only by drawing upon a considerable variety of evidence can we be certain that our judgment is well-rounded and fair to the young person.

It isn't only teachers and school officials who sometimes overemphasize test scores. A bright seventeen-year-old girl was telling me recently about a boy she had begun to date: "He didn't pay much attention to me at first, but then he asked me what my test scores were. I told him and his whole attitude changed for the better." It's a chilling anecdote on several counts, most of all perhaps in its implication that meritocracy isn't coming—it's here.

Another important rule is that diagnosis of the young person's aptitudes and achievements should be a continuing process. It would be misleading to suggest that repeated appraisals must be made because we expect major variations in the youngster's aptitudes from year to year. The truth is that his aptitudes will probably remain pretty stable. But at any given age level, the test scores or grades or other measures may not be a precise reflection of his aptitude or achievement. Repeated appraisals enrich and stabilize the diagnosis.

Still another important rule is that crucial judgments on the youngster's future should not be based entirely on intellectual gifts. We have pointed out that traits of personality and character are of central importance in the child's later performance. These should carry due weight in any decisions made. This is so obvious that one might wonder why it needs to be mentioned—but the plain fact is that most current selection procedures neglect the point altogether. The easiest, laziest thing to do is to sort out youngsters by their test scores and forget the complications. Teachers should not only combat this laziness; they should be constantly on the alert for the other attributes that promise to strengthen and guide performance in later life. I shall point out in a later chapter that there are many kinds of human excellence. To the extent that we insist on sorting individuals out on the basis of one or two scores that sum up one dimension of human performance, we are constricting reality and denying the richness of human possibilities.

A somewhat comparable oversimplification is evident in the unimaginative and often snobbish "credentialism" that is practiced in many of our leading professional offices and executive suites today. Did the candidate get his A.B. from one of the "right" colleges, his M.B.A. from one of the "right" business schools? It is said of many a leader of the bar that he couldn't get an interview in his own firm today.

Diagnosis of an individual's future capacity to perform remains a hazardous undertaking. There are mysteries in individual development that we are far from understanding. No stone should be left unturned to insure that decisions are based on a wide range of evidence, carefully gathered and sifted. Through repeated appraisals of the youngster at various ages, through the use of a variety of measures, through the pooling of many judgments, we are simply acknowledging the complexity of the subject and proceeding with caution.

It cannot be emphasized too often that the greatest enemy of sound and fair selection processes today is the apparent simplicity and efficiency involved in assigning a single score (or pair of scores) to each youngster. The rapid and efficient handling of large numbers of individuals exerts tremendous pressure toward oversimplified diagnoses, toward the summation of individual attributes in a single index number, and toward complete dependence on that number as a key to the individual's fate. Considerations of efficiency must not be allowed to distort our diagnoses or to narrow our conception of talent.

No doubt the course of action I am recommending would be more time-consuming and expensive than current procedures. But if we allow considerations of efficiency to falsify our assessments and narrow our conception of talent, we shall see, finally, an uncontrollable public rejection of the tests.

CHAPTER EIGHT

Facts and Fancies about Talent

THE STRATEGY A SOCIETY ADOPTS to deal with differences in ability may depend in part on its views concerning the hereditary nature of such differences. As we shall see, the genetic facts cannot be decisive for social policy; but in the past, certain widely held views concerning heredity have played a powerful role in buttressing social policy with respect to differences in ability.

In societies of hereditary privilege it was believed, of course, that the social strata corresponded to differences in human quality. And since these differences are hereditary, the argument ran, the stratification is hereditary. It is always startling to the American traveling in a society that still has strong elements of stratification to discover that though the lower classes may resent certain social inequalities, they more than half-accept the ideology that supports those inequalities. I recall my own astonishment as a young American soldier in Italy in 1944 when an elderly Italian servant (not my servant!) patiently explained to me that the social hierarchy was based on the unshakable facts of human heredity.

As the democracies emerged, the idea that differences in social status were due to differences in hereditary quality was, of course, rejected. But even in the democracies the notion refused to die altogether. Herbert Spencer, the nineteenth-century English philosopher, believed that the poor were "unfit" and should be eliminated. Not many accepted so stern a view, but it was tempting for the rich and well-born to suppose that the stratification existing at any given moment was rooted in their own genetic superiority.

In the same spirit it was easy, during the heaviest periods of immigration to this country, to believe that the latest crop of arrivals simply lacked the native ability to rise from ignorance and poverty. Thus H. G. Wells wrote in 1906:

> I doubt very much if America is going to assimilate all that she is taking in now; much more do I doubt that she will assimilate the still greater inflow of the coming years. . . . I believe that if things go on as they are going, the great mass of them will remain a very low lower class—will remain largely illiterate industrial peasants.[1]

He could not have imagined that from the descendants of that "very low lower class" would arise statesmen, artists, capitalists, and professionals of great competence and distinction.

As I pointed out earlier, the view that the social strata coincided with a natural hierarchy of ability received a shattering blow with the development of relatively objective measures of mental performance. The earliest extensive use of objective tests, in World War I, made it clear that intelligence was widely distributed in the population and that there were rich resources of ability at every social level. This is a fact never mentioned by those who regard testing as the instrument of a repressive elite.

Though the tests made it clear that mental performance did not follow the lines of social stratification, they did not settle the question of whether ability was hereditary. For years this was one of the liveliest topics of debate among research people in psychology—and it is still capable of stirring intense argument.

It is sufficiently controversial as a purely intellectual question. It becomes more so because of its implications for social and political theory. Scholars whose weighing of the evidence leads them to believe that heredity is the dominant factor in intelligence find that this conclusion endears them to some conservative elements in the society and gains the hostility of certain left-wing thinkers. Lewis Terman, a pioneer in the testing of intelligence, was bitterly criticized by Soviet writers for placing heavy emphasis on heredity as a determinant of intelligence. On the other hand, individuals whose weighing of the evidence persuades them that environment is more important than heredity find themselves applauded by those who want very much to believe that all intellectual inequalities between individuals are due to social inequalities.

It is not easy to settle an intellectual question when people have a powerful emotional stake in one or another outcome.[2] The most experienced and objective students of these matters are cautious in asking how much of behavior is determined by heredity and how much by environment as though one were

asking how many eggs and how much milk went into a pud-
ding. The question oversimplifies an enormously complex interaction and treats as separate and self-contained ingredients
two factors that are essentially inseparable. Typical of the caution of experts is the judgment expressed in the authoritative
psychology text by Atkinson, Atkinson, and Hilgard: "Heredity
clearly has an effect on intelligence, but the degree of this
effect is uncertain."[3]

There is no doubt that the striking differences in environment that exist do have an effect upon intellectual performance. Some youngsters find themselves in a stimulating and
instructive environment from the first days of infancy, with
intelligent adults giving them immeasurable help; other young
people grow up in a barren and impoverished environment.

There is evidence that such differences do affect intelligence as measured by tests. But there is also considerable
evidence that the effect of environmental circumstances on
ability is limited. This has been demonstrated in studies of
identical twins reared apart. It is also suggested by the relative
stability of individual rankings in test scores. If environmental
circumstances powerfully affect the rankings, one would not
expect them to be a very stable measure. They are far from
constant, and in any substantial batch of cases it is possible to
point to some marked changes in individual rankings over a
period of years. But considering the wide range of environ-
ments through which human beings pass, the remarkable thing
about the rankings is their relative stability.

The precise degree of heritability of intelligence, as measured by tests, will continue to be the subject of debate among
experts. But the majority of modern workers in the field have
a balanced view of the question.

Lay people are not so deeply concerned to achieve clarity

in matters of theory. They want to know what it all means for them and for their children. And the truth is that most experts are in reasonable agreement (though they might never admit it) as to what it means for the layman.

When we examine the appropriate social policy to be adopted, we are faced with a simpler task than the behavior theorists are faced with. Precise answers on the question are not necessary. Even if environment were a modest factor—and it is much more than that—in determining ability to perform, social policy would necessarily emphasize the importance of taking this factor into account. Even if only two or three children in ten might gain in intellectual effectiveness through a more favorable environment, we would still be bound to make the effort. Whatever the verdict on the fine points of the technical argument, our job is to make the most of each child's potentialities.

The other major factor in social policy must be a straightforward admission of the fact that individuals do differ greatly in their capacities, and each must be enabled to develop the talent that is in him. *Whether individual differences in ability are innate or are due to environmental differences, we must deal with them imaginatively and constructively.*

If we are going to develop a sensible approach to the encouragement of talent, we shall have to dispose of various myths surrounding the talented individual.

There is, for example, an old wives' tale to the effect that most highly gifted children "burn themselves out" and never amount to anything as adults. The companion belief is that great men were almost invariably either dull or fractious children. Neither is true.

There is something immensely satisfying about both beliefs and it is a pity to explode them. What could be more comforting to ordinary mortals than the thought that Winston Churchill was an unpromising youngster? Or that Charles Darwin had trouble in school? Or that William Faulkner was a poor student? But it has been demonstrated over and over that youngsters who show early promise tend to perform better in later life than youngsters who do not show early promise.

And research on the early careers of people of great ability has demonstrated that as a rule their gifts were observable even in childhood. Alexander Pope was twelve years old—junior high-school-age in this country—when he penned the melancholy lines.

> Thus let me live unseen, unknown
> Thus unlamented let me die,
> Steal from the world, and not a stone
> Tell where I lie.

Mozart learned to play the clavier between three and four years of age. Carlyle was only eleven months old and had never spoken a word when, hearing another child in the household cry, he sat up and said, "What ails wee Jock?"[4]

There are, of course, plenty of exceptions. And there should be. Success involves more than talent, and some individuals simply lack the character or motivation to make the most of their talent. When I was in college, a professor said of one of my more indolent classmates, "He has great gifts but he's too lazy to unwrap them."

But on the whole, promise is usually borne out. The classic research in this field is the work of Lewis Terman, who in the 1920s selected a group of 1,000 gifted children for long-term study.[5] Repeated follow-up studies over the decades provide impressive evidence of continued high performance.

Another popular misconception is the notion that great talent is usually highly specific. The research evidence indicates that gifted individuals generally have many talents rather than a single talent. If the individual is promising in one line, the best guess is that he will be promising in a number of lines.

But talented individuals do not develop their gifts along all the lines open to them, so in later life they may seem less broadly talented than they actually are. Some narrowing is inevitable. There are limitations of time and energy. And there is a "tyranny of talent" that tends to force the narrowing of anyone with extraordinarily high ability in a specific line. Once the talent is discovered it is often so highly rewarded that the individual is apt to neglect (or not to discover) other gifts. With all those clavichord recitals at age seven, Mozart could not have had much time for exploration of his other talents. Such one-sided development may be essential to the highest reaches of performance, and it might be foolish to try to prevent it in people of great promise. But anyone responsible for very gifted young people would do well to assist them in exploring the full range of their talents where possible, and to postpone at least for a time the tyrannical narrowing down.

Finally, there is the myth that the extremely gifted individual is unstable. In this case the myth is particularly hard to disprove because of the vivid examples that seem to support it. One thinks of Van Gogh cutting off his ear, of Poe's alcoholism, of Nietzsche's incoherent end. But again, the weight of solid evidence is in the other direction. Whenever systematic data have been gathered on a wide range of gifted individuals it has been found that they are not more unstable than the less gifted. The advantage is more likely to be in the other direction.

Talent and Motivation

Dan, who was twelve years old and the best ballplayer in his school, was undergoing a psychological interview. The psychologist said, "What is the thing you feel you need to change to be the kind of person you'd like to be?" Dan replied, "Learn to spell. Learn to throw a knuckler that hops."[6]

If all young people were as capable as Dan of putting first things first, some of the perplexing problems facing American education would resolve themselves.

Everyone agrees that motivation is a powerful ingredient in performance. Talent without motivation is inert and of little use to the world. Lewis Terman and Catherine Cox found that historical geniuses were characterized not only by very high intelligence but by the desire to excel, by perseverance in the face of obstacles, by zeal in the exercise of their gifts.[7]

Some people may have greatness thrust upon them. Very few have excellence thrust upon them. They achieve it. They do not achieve it unwittingly, by "doin' what comes naturally"; and they don't stumble into it in the course of amusing themselves. All excellence involves discipline and tenacity of purpose.

Unfortunately we are a long way from understanding the complexities of individual motivation. We understand very imperfectly the inner pressures to excel that are present in some children and absent in others. We don't really know why, from earliest years, some individuals seem indomitable while others are tossed about by events like the bird in a badminton game. Why do some individuals experience defeat early and live out their lives in resignation, while others seem capable of endless renewal, rising from defeat, learning and growing, constantly discovering new resources of energy and spirit?

If we are concerned with the full development of our young people, we must give attention to these motivational factors that lead people to level off short of their full ceiling. If we learn how to salvage any respectable fraction of these, we will have unlocked a great storehouse of talent.[8]

CHAPTER NINE

Education as a Sorting-out Process

VERY SCHOOL MORNING some 44 million American children gulp their breakfast, grab their books, slam the front door, and dash off to class. Among them go not one but several future presidents of the United States, a handful of future Supreme Court justices, and dozens of future cabinet members.

The Rigors of Sorting Out

Educational systems have always had a great deal to do with the eventual roles of the students who pass through them. It was said of German university students at the end of the nineteenth century that one-third broke down, one-third went to the devil, and the remaining third went on to govern Europe.

Americans believe that promise should be recognized at whatever level in society it occurs. They like to think that those future presidents dashing off to school may come from any walk of life.

But as education becomes increasingly effective in pulling the able youngster to the top, it becomes an increasingly rugged sorting-out process for everyone concerned. The schools are the golden avenue of opportunity for able youngsters; but they are also the arena in which less able youngsters discover their limitations. This thought rarely occurred to the generations of Americans who dreamed of universal education. They saw the beauty of a system in which young people could go as far as their ability and ambition would take them, without obstacles of money, social standing, religion, or race. They didn't reflect on the pain involved for those who lacked the necessary ability. Yet pain there is and must be.

Although the American people generally have never explicitly faced up to the realities of the sorting-out process, they have demonstrated in many ways that they sense the painfulness of it. Even the most casual glance at our educational system will reveal our great reluctance to put labels on individual differences in general capacity. Consider the broad interpretation we give to the phrase "college education." When young people are graduated from high school we discuss those going on to college as though they were a homogeneous lot, all headed for a similar experience. But the truth is that they are quietly but fairly effectively sorted into different paths.

Anyone who has enjoyed a behind-the-scenes view of how a good high school deals with its graduating seniors is familiar with the process. Consider the work of Miss L., an assistant principal. One of her tasks is to advise the girls who want to go on to college. Miss L. has a clear impression of every girl in the senior class. She has known most of them since they entered high school. She knows what subjects they like and what subjects they find easy. She knows how hard they work and what their hopes are for college. And she knows a great deal about colleges—what the entrance requirements are, and what kind of girl is likely to be happy in what college.

The students need not listen to Miss L.'s advice but usually do. She sends her college-bound girls out along widely diverging pathways—to colleges of the highest possible standards, to colleges of moderate difficulty, and so on down to colleges that may be ranked lower academically than the best high schools. But though she must appraise accurately the relative standings of colleges and the relative capacities of students, Miss L. will usually not make these appraisals explicit. She will not say bluntly that the student is of limited ability and therefore should go to a second-class college. She will tell the parents that their youngster is not "a natural student" or "not one of those with a tremendous drive to get grades" and therefore should probably go to one of the colleges "where the entrance requirements are not quite so exacting."

Dr. and Mrs. Roger Barker, American psychologists, made an intensive study of the daily lives of children in the small town of Leyburn, England.[1] One of the many striking differences they found between Leyburn and a comparable American town was the degree of candor about differences in ability. In England when a schoolchild gave a foolish answer the teacher was likely to respond with a candid appraisal of his performance and even of his native capacity. It was not at all unthinkable for the teacher to make some remark such as, "Johnny, sit down—you're not up to this."[2]

Such candor is outside the experience of most American

observers. The American teacher might say that Johnny had not studied his lesson, or that Johnny was lazy, or that Johnny was inattentive. She might impugn his cooperativeness, or his ambition, or his knowledge. But she would rarely indicate that his ability was limited. We much prefer not to discuss such matters at all. Indeed, we are capable of devising rather elaborate institutional arrangements to get around the painful business of telling Johnny that he is not smart.

One point of view to take toward this national peculiarity is that we have developed a ridiculous squeamishness about such matters. But the reason we do not like to label differences in capacity is that individual capacity holds a uniquely important place in our scheme of things.

Ours is one of those societies in which performance is a primary determinant of status. What young men and women can "deliver" in the way of performance is a major factor in how far they can rise in the world. In a stratified society, performance is not an important factor in establishing status, so individuals can afford to be less than deeply concerned about their capacity. After entertaining a visiting monarch, President Lyndon B. Johnson once said, "He's the dumbest king I ever met. I didn't know they made kings that dumb."[3]

If you're a king it doesn't matter. But for every step that a society takes away from a stratified system and toward a system in which performance is the chief determinant of status, individuals will be increasingly concerned about their capacity.

There are all kinds of individual capacity. That is a point to which we shall return. But for complex reasons, Americans see appraisals of "intelligence," however defined, as total judgments on the individual and as central to his or her self-esteem. Some critics note that we discriminate nicely between excellence and mediocrity in athletics but refuse to be similarly precise about differences in intelligence; and they attribute this to the fact that we are more seriously concerned with athletic ability than we are with intelligence. Nothing could be farther from the truth. We can afford, emotionally speaking, to be coldly objective in judgments of athletic ability precisely because we do not take these as total judgments on the individual or as central to his self-esteem.

A major feature of our dealing with levels of ability is what I shall call our principle of multiple chances. The European system used to separate youngsters at ten or eleven years of age on the basis of ability and then prepare some for the university, others for less demanding levels of education. This was in some respects an efficient procedure; and there were critics here at home who thought we should have a similar system. But in recent years some European countries have modified the system, and we have never found it attractive. In the American view, it presents a host of difficulties, only one of which need be noted here: early separation of the gifted and the less gifted violates our principle of multiple chances.

We believe that youngsters should have many successive opportunities to discover themselves. We postpone as long as possible any final closing of the door on the individual's chances. A college senior, teetering on the brink of failure and studying for his final examinations, said to me, "Dad says it's my last chance. So far that makes it the seventh last chance." It is a unique feature of our system that "late bloomers" may dawdle or occupy themselves with other than educational objectives until as late as eighteen or nineteen years of age (roughly first or second year of college) and still (provided that they are able) not only obtain a college education but go on to become professional people.

Some years ago a friend in a Western city mentioned a Dr. S. to me and described him as "the best internist in town." The name was familiar and I asked if he were the S. who had attended the University of California in the 1930s. He was. But the image my memory supplied was not that of a brilliant pre-med student. It was of a pleasantly aimless young man with no interest in studies and no goal more serious than to hold his position as shortstop on the baseball team. I mentioned this to my friend, and he grinned. "That was S. all right; but in his junior year he woke up, and after that nothing could stop him."

That is the sort of story we all find pleasing, but it should not mislead us. It is rare for aimless young men with no interest in studies to turn into leading physicians. And S. was fortunate to have graduated from high school fifty years ago. Today he would have greater difficulty getting into a good university, and far greater trouble getting in a good medical school. Even a very prosperous society cannot afford to spend large sums allowing such youngsters to loaf their way through a prolonged adolescence.

It is not only the late bloomer who benefits from the principle of multiple chances. Children who have grown up in homes barren of educational or cultural influences may require a longer exposure to school before they wake up.

The practice followed by many of our public universities of accepting all high-school graduates who apply and then weeding them out in large numbers during freshman year is partly a response to political pressures. But it is warmly defended by many in terms of our principle of multiple chances. It can be argued that it is better to let students try and fail—and in failing discover their own inadequacy—than to tell them they are not good enough to try. Of course, the answer would be that such youngsters have already had many chances to prove themselves before they reach college. True, says the defender of the system, but the extraordinary symbolic importance that college education is gaining in our society may require that the youngster be given one further try. It can be argued that allowing young people to discover their own inadequacies is pretty sensible social strategy.

The powerful impulse in the American people to temper the wind to the less able youngster makes critics of American education grind their teeth in despair. And their despair is not wholly unjustified. But no one has a right to join the critics until he has thought long and hard about the authentic difficulty of the social problem the American system must solve. The sorting out of individuals according to ability is very nearly the most delicate and difficult process our society has to face.

Those who receive the most education have considerably increased the likelihood that they will move into the society's key jobs. Thus the question "Who should go to college?" translates itself into the more fateful question "Who is going to manage the society?" That is not the kind of question one can treat lightly or cavalierly. It is the kind of question that wars have been fought over.

It must never be forgotten that a person born to low status in a rigidly stratified society has a far more acceptable self-image than the person who loses out in our free competition of talent. In an older society, the humble member of society can attribute his lowly status to God's will, to the ancient order of things, or to a corrupt and tyrannous government. But if a society sorts people out with reasonable efficiency according to their gifts, many who end up low on the scale will be forced to face up to their own inadequacies—and that can be a bitter pill.

There are, of course, gifted individuals who fail to achieve high status because they lack character or because they simply refuse the terms of the competition. But for the purposes of this discussion, let us focus on the problem of those of low ability.

An example may clarify the problem. During World War II a military commander told me about a situation he had encountered in the small unit under his command. This unit had been organized for special work and included an unusual number of highly intelligent enlisted men. An opportunity arose to send men to officers' candidate school, and the commander set it as his high-minded goal to recommend every one of his enlisted men who was properly qualified. He screened them and identified those of officer caliber, and every one that he recommended was accepted for officer's candidate school.

What were the consequences? The morale of the remaining enlisted men disintegrated. Investigation revealed that the screening process had left them without a shred of self-esteem. They were relatively happy as long as they could say to themselves that they were enlisted men because it's all a matter of luck or because this is an unjust world, or because the military services do not value ability. But the commanding officer's scrupulous search for talent had deprived them of those comfortable defenses. They had no place to hide. It now seemed clear to all concerned that they were enlisted men because that was where they belonged.

If they had known the flaws in most selection procedures, they might have been less depressed. But the point is clear enough. There are social hazards in rigorous selection. Yet we must engage in such selection. As we shall see, there are ways to do it wisely.

CHAPTER TEN

The School's Hard Assignment

The High School

THE ARENA in which the rigors of sorting out are most clearly visible is the high school. It was not always so. Up through the early years of the twentieth century the function of the high school was college preparatory, and those who entered its doors were a fairly homogeneous lot. It wasn't until 1930 that the census showed over 50 percent of young people between 14 and 17 years of age in high school. Today roughly 95 percent of that age group are in attendance.

In the early years of the century, when students who were not necessarily headed for college began to flood into the high schools, major changes were inevitable. The old curriculum seemed ill fitted to serve the needs of the newly diverse student body, and it was partially discarded, partially watered down. During the 1920s the schools added vocational courses and many other programs designed to serve (and hold the attention of) the less bookish youngsters now entering—courses in health, consumer education, the wise use of leisure, and so on. "Life adjustment education" was the key phrase.

Criticism of the new direction was derisive, but to many of the school people who were making the changes it was not only necessary but exciting. They saw themselves as "democratizing" the schools and relating them to the community. They talked of infusing the schools with practical purposes, e.g., courses in citizenship, in economic understanding, in ethics. Some said they were making the school an instrument of social change.

One element in the effort to make the high school a more livable environment for the non-college preparatory youngster was to blunt the edge of competition where possible. For some educators then (the 1920s) and now, this effort had deep philosophical roots. As a counterbalance to the American zest for competitive performance, there has been throughout much of our history a certain number of Americans who rejected, on philosophical grounds, the endless striving and the scramble for rewards. This philosophy, as applied to the schools, favored cooperative rather than competitive activity and sought to deemphasize promotions on merit. It deplored the marking system not only because it exacerbated competition but because it offered extrinsic rewards (i.e., grades) for something (i.e., learning) that should be its own reward. The general idea was that no child should fail. Unfortunately this attempt to diminish the rigors of competitiveness too often involved an elimination of performance standards of any kind.

As indicated earlier, when the high schools began to accept

large numbers of young people who were not necessarily headed for college, change in the high school itself became inevitable. The effort to broaden and diversify the whole approach to education had many good consequences. It opened windows and let some fresh breezes into the schoolroom; and more important, it brought the high school through a huge and historic transition.

But there were less attractive consequences. Some of the new programs were ill-conceived, some were silly. Perhaps the worst of the consequences was the tendency to underestimate the students who were not (then) classified as college material. In their behalf virtually all of the old basic subjects were either rejected or diluted beyond recognition. The school people wanted so intensely to be "democratic" that they ended up being patronizing, indeed at times anti-intellectual, in their turning away from book knowledge and knowledge for its own sake. The well-worn joke of the time was of the college admissions officer who asked the applicant from a progressive school whether he had taken European History. "Oh, yes—twice!" was the reply. "Once in sand and once in clay."

These early excesses, many of them under the banner of "progressive education," led to a reaction. Indeed the history of the past three-quarters of a century in education has seemed to some observers to resemble nothing so much as a madly swinging pendulum. In one phase there are experiments with less intellectual fare, and then a "back to basics" movement; a phase of permissiveness and then discipline; "social promotion" and then basic competency tests; diversification and then a return to the core curriculum.

But it has not all been as faddish and trend-ridden as it may have seemed. Many important innovations were introduced on both swings of the pendulum.

The successive swings reveal several dimensions of conflict in educational philosophy; but the one that is of overriding importance for the present discussion stems from the fact that the high school has diverse functions that are not easily reconciled.

The root question is "How can the school provide *all* young people with certain basics necessary to their common citizenship and at the same time give them the diverse opportunities and treatment that their differential abilities require?" The problem is hard enough in its own right but made all the harder by issues of race, language, and economic deprivation.

If the swings of the pendulum have been excessive at times and the debate more embittered than one might wish, it is because there are extreme and polarizing elements on both sides of the debate.

On the side of quality, the best proponents care deeply about standards and solid subject matter, seek to challenge and stretch the student, and believe that with appropriate adjustments these are suitable goals for students at every level of ability. Unfortunately, also on the side of quality are some who really care only about the college preparatory students and (whether they admit it or not) look down on all the others. Not surprisingly, they give an unpleasant tone to the debate.

On the side of equality, the best proponents care deeply about the economically deprived and about the student of lesser ability—but fully recognize the need for rigorous college preparatory programs. Unfortunately, also on the side of equality are some who are profoundly anti-intellectual, anti-subject matter, and anti-discipline.

The worst in each group polarize the argument. Our task is to bring into coalition the best in each group to fashion a workable synthesis. A concern for equality and a concern for the pursuit of excellence at every level are not mutually exclusive. When they appear (or are) mutually threatening, it is because the tension between the two has been mismanaged.

Major studies by Ernest Boyer[1] and by John Goodlad[2] suggest that we are moving toward sensible middle-of-the-road solutions to the problem. But unresolved difficulties remain.

Most schools pursue some means of providing differing course programs for students at different levels of ability. Some do it very subtly, offering the same basic courses to all (but taught at different levels of difficulty), offering good vocational electives for the student who is not headed for college, good math, science, and foreign language courses for those who are —and accomplishing it all in such a way as to minimize invidious distinctions among students.

Other schools create quite visible "tracks" with virtually no bridging courses. Naturally, students are well aware of the sorting out that has occurred.

James B. Conant was famous for his insistence that the differential treatment of different groups should all take place in a single school—a comprehensive high school in which social, athletic, and student government activities could serve as binding elements among all levels of ability. Bearing in mind the inevitable tensions we described earlier—tensions that our kind of society can never escape—one can think of the comprehensive high school as an important means of creating social cohesion.

Samuel Lewis, first superintendent of common schools in Ohio, wrote in 1836:

Take fifty lads in a neighborhood, including rich and poor—send them in childhood to the same school—let them join in the same sports, read and spell in the same classes, until their different circumstances fix their business for life: some go to the field, some to the mechanic's shop, some to merchandize: one becomes eminent at the bar, another in the pulpit: some become wealthy; the majority live on with a mere competency—a few are reduced to beggary! But let the most eloquent orator, that ever mounted a western stump, attempt to prejudice the minds of one part against the other—and so far from succeeding, the poorest of the whole would consider himself insulted.[3]

The comprehensive high school is still the norm. But the trend toward separate schools for different groups, though still modest, is unmistakable. So-called "magnet schools" and "alternative schools" within a school district are becoming increasingly popular to serve special groups and interests. And private schools flourish, serving in addition to their traditional purposes the more recent purpose of "white flight," a subject no one really likes to talk about. Finally, schools in the wealthy suburbs, though they have the appearance of the comprehensive high school, are sociologically closer to the private prep schools, as I mentioned earlier.

We have given sufficient emphasis to the painfulness of the sorting-out process. We now know that when we overreact to this painfulness, we tumble into a ditch on the other side of the road. And that ditch is no less deep. At times our desire to protect young people from invidious comparisons has produced serious confusion in educational objectives and a dangerous erosion of standards. Such consequences, whether rare or frequent, are a legitimate cause for concern.

There is concern today, for example, that we have worried all too little about the youngster of unusual gifts. It is true. But for the sake of our own dignity, let it not be just another swing of the pendulum that will reach the end of its arc and return. The way to prevent that result is to pursue our concern for the gifted without castigating ourselves for having given unprecedented attention to the average or below average youngster. Our kind of society demands the maximum development of individual potentialities *at every level of ability;* and we would be very foolish indeed if we were to let a renewed interest in the gifted youngster lead to neglect of everyone else. Martin Luther said that humanity is like a drunken peasant who is always ready to fall from his horse on one side or the other, and in that respect we Americans are all too human. We must learn to see the achievements and shortcomings of our educational system in some sort of embracing perspective that will permit us to repair one defect without creating others.

The traditional democratic invitation to individuals to achieve the best that is in them requires that we provide each youngster with the particular kind of education suited to his or her special abilities. That is the only sense in which equality of opportunity can mean anything. The good society is not one that ignores individual differences but one that deals with them wisely and humanely.

What the Schools Need

There has been plenty of evidence that the schools are in serious trouble. A series of influential studies[4] released in 1983 documented that fact. Falling achievement scores, students inadequately prepared in basic subjects, teachers incapable of meeting minimum standards in their own subjects—the indictments are familiar. The studies make many recommendations that are of unquestionable value: better selection and training of teachers, better leadership and management by superintendents and above all principals, measures to ensure the acquiring basic competence in key subjects—and so on.

The studies also offered more novel ideas, some of them quite good, some in the gimmick category.

With such a wealth of recommendations before us, it may

be foolhardy to comment. But without going over well-plowed ground, I would simply emphasize a few basic points.

1) The best thing about the burst of reform in the 1980s is that it brought the public's wavering attention back to the schools. Americans care deeply about the schools; but their minds wander. The basic requirement for effective functioning of the schools is that the public be concerned and involved. As Willy Loman's wife said in *Death of a Salesman*, "Attention must be paid."

2) The schools must be adequately funded. Various tax rebellions have pushed many school systems to the wall financially. One can understand how such things may happen—but from the standpoint of public policy it is insanity. John Adams, in a letter to a friend, wrote, "The whole people must take upon themselves the education of the whole people, and must be willing to bear the expense of it."[5] In discussing this problem today, observers often note that with growth in the aging population there is an increasing proportion of voters who have no children in school and therefore have no concern for the schools. I am not willing to believe that any considerable number of older people share that despicable attitude. Did they not benefit from an earlier generation of taxpayers? Is the future of America not their concern too?

3) The public should undertake with enthusiasm the task of improving their schools but should bear in mind that the schools have been heavily battered by the successive storms of change. . They have lived through urban disintegration, major demographic changes, court decisions mandating profound shifts in practice, and long periods of public indifference and nonsupport. One need not excuse the schools for clear evidence of weak performance. But let us approach the task of improving them with a nurturing regard for institutions that

have lived through a lot—and a regard, too, for teachers, who must ultimately carry the battle for school improvement. As Fred Hechinger has pointed out, "There is no lack of generals who are calling for a campaign to improve the schools. . . . What is lacking is an army of teachers trained to fight the battle for reforms."[6]

4) Referring to the earlier discussion of quality and equality, let us take the discussion out of the hands of the polarizers and build an educational system that serves each in terms of his or her talents, stretching each, challenging each, demanding of all the best that is in them.

CHAPTER ELEVEN

College and the Alternatives

Who Should Go to College?

A￼LL OF the conflicting and confusing notions that Americans have concerning equality, excellence, and the encouragement of talent are reflected in some of the discussions of who should go to college.

One hears the phrase "Everyone has a right to go to college." It is easy to dispose of this position in its extreme form. There are some youngsters whose mental retardation is so severe that they cannot enter the first grade. There are a number of youngsters out of every hundred whose mental limitations make it impossible for them to get as far as junior high school. There are others who can progress through high school only if they are placed in special programs that take into account their academic limitations.

It is true that some who fall in this group would have ranked higher had it not been for social and economic handicaps. But there are many children whose academic limitations cannot possibly be traced to social deprivation. Children with severe intellectual limitations appear not infrequently in families that are able to give them every advantage and to explore exhaustively the possibilities of treatment or special tutoring. Such children can be helped, but the hope that any major change can be accomplished in their academic limitations is usually doomed to disappointment.

With each higher grade an increasing number of youngsters find it difficult or impossible to keep up with the work. Many never complete high school.

What percent of the college-age group should go to college? There is in fact no limit to how many can go if we design our colleges to suit our intentions. Less than 1 percent of the college-age population are qualified to attend the California Institute of Technology. There are other colleges where 10, 20, 40 or 60 percent of the college-age population are qualified to attend.

It would be possible to create institutions with standards so low that 90 percent of the college-age population could qualify. In order to do so it would be necessary to establish institutions at about the intellectual level of summer camps. If it were certain that almost all of the eighteen-to-twenty-two-year-old population could benefit by full-time attendance at "colleges" of this sort, one would be duty-bound to explore the matter further. But one must look with extreme skepticism upon the notion that all high-school graduates can profit by continued formal schooling. There is no question that they can profit by continued *education*. But the character of this education will vary from one youngster to the next. Some will profit by continued book learning; others by some kind of vocational training; still others by learning on the job. Others may require other kinds of growth experiences. Educating everyone up to the limit of his or her ability does not mean sending everyone to college.

To the extent that that is a bitter pill—as it is for many—we are all at fault. We have placed a wholly false emphasis on college education. In Virginia they tell the story of the kindly Episcopal minister who was asked whether the Episcopal Church was the only path of salvation. The minister shook his head—a bit sadly. "No, there are other paths," he said, and then added, "but no gentleman would choose them." Some of our attitudes toward college education verge dangerously on the same position.

As a result, we lead youngsters to assume that the only useful learning and growth come from attending college, listening to professors talk from platforms, and reproducing required information on occasions called examinations. This is an extremely constricting notion.

In the case of the youngster who is not very talented academically, forced continuance of education may simply prolong a situation in which he is doomed to failure. Many a youngster of low ability has been kept on pointlessly in a school that did not prepare him to earn a living and undermined his confidence beyond repair. That is not a sensible way to conserve human resources.

Properly understood, a college or university offers *one kind of further education, suitable to those whose capacities fit them for that kind of education.* It should not be regarded as the sole means of establishing one's human worth. It should not be seen as the unique key to happiness, self-respect, and inner confidence.

We have all done our bit to foster these misconceptions. And the root of the difficulty is our bad habit of assuming that the goal of life is "success," defining success in terms of high material rewards or high personal attainment in the world's eyes. Today attendance at college has become virtually a prerequisite to success so defined. So that it becomes, in the false value framework we have created, the only passport to a meaningful life. No wonder our colleges are crowded.

The crowding in our colleges is less regrettable than the confusion in our values. *Human dignity and worth should be assessed only in terms of those qualities of mind and spirit that are within the reach of every human being.* If we make the assumption that college is the sole cradle of human dignity, need we be surprised that everyone wants to be rocked in that cradle?

This is not to say that we should not value achievement. We should value it exceedingly. It is simply to say that achievement should not be confused with human worth. Our recognition of the dignity and worth of the individual is based upon moral imperatives and should be of universal application. In other words, everyone has a "right" to that recognition. Being a college graduate involves qualities of mind that can never be universally possessed. Not everyone has a right to be a college graduate, any more than everyone has the right to run a four-minute mile.

What we are really seeking is what James Conant had in mind when he said that the American people are concerned not only for equality of opportunity but equality of respect. Every human being who lives within the society's legal and ethical framework is entitled to respect regardless of his ability or wealth or status. John Rawls lists "a sense of one's own worth" as one of the chief primary goods.[1]

The Need for Institutional Diversity

But a scaling down of our emphasis on college education is only part of the answer. Another important part of the answer must be a greatly increased emphasis upon individual differences, upon many kinds of talent, upon the immensely varied ways in which individual potentialities may be realized.

One step is to welcome diversity in our higher educational system to correspond to the diversity of the clientele. There is no other way to handle within one system the enormously disparate human capacities, levels of preparedness, and motivations that flow into our colleges and universities.

But we cannot hope to create or to maintain such diversity unless we honor the various aspects of that diversity. Each of the different kinds of institution has a significant part to play in creating the total pattern, and each should be allowed to play its role with honor and recognition if it performs well. No institution should be ashamed of its distinctive features so long as it is doing something that contributes importantly to the total pattern, and so long as it is striving for excellence in performance. The highly selective, small liberal arts college should not be afraid to remain small. The large urban institution should not be ashamed that it is large. The technical institute should not be apologetic about being a technical institute. Each institution should pride itself on the role that it has chosen to play and on the special contribution that it brings to the total pattern of American higher education.

Such diversity is the only means of achieving quality within a framework of quantity. For we must not forget the primacy of our concern for excellence. We must have diversity, but we must also expect that every institution which makes up that diversity will be striving, in its own way, for excellence. This may require a new way of thinking about excellence in higher education—a conception that would be applicable in terms of the objectives of the institution. As things now stand, the word "excellence" is all too often reserved for the dozen or two dozen institutions that stand at the very zenith of our higher education in terms of faculty distinction, selectivity of students, and difficulty of curriculum. In these terms it is simply impossible to speak of a junior college, for example, as excellent. Yet sensible people can easily conceive of excellence in a junior college.

The traditionalist might say, "Of course! Let Princeton create a junior college and one would have an institution of unquestionable excellence!" That may be correct, but it may also lead us down precisely the wrong path. If Princeton Junior College were excellent, it might not be excellent in the most important way that a community college can be excellent. It might simply be a truncated version of Princeton. A comparably meaningless result would be achieved if General Motors tried to add to its line of low-priced cars by marketing the front half of a Cadillac.

In higher education as in everything else there is no excellent performance without high morale. No morale, no excellence! And in a great many of our colleges and universities the most stubborn enemy of high morale has been a kind of hopelessness on the part of both administration and faculty—hopelessness about ever achieving distinction as an institution. Not only are such attitudes a corrosive influence on morale, they make it virtually certain that the institution will never achieve even an excellence within its reach. For there is a kind of excellence within the reach of every institution.

In short, we reject the notion that excellence is something that can only be experienced in the most rarified strata of higher education. It may be experienced at every level and in every serious kind of education. And we must *demand* excellence in every form that higher education takes. We should not ask it lightly or amiably or good-naturedly; we should demand it vigorously and insistently. We should assert that a stubborn striving for excellence is the price of admission to reputable educational circles, and that those institutions not character-ized by this striving are the slatterns of higher education.

We must make the same challenging demands of students. We must never make the insolent and degrading assumption that young people unfit for the most demanding fields of intel-lectual endeavor are incapable of rigorous attention to *some sort of standards.* It is an appalling error to assume—as some of our institutions seem to have assumed—that young men and women incapable of the highest standards of intellectual excel-lence are incapable of any standards whatsoever and can prop-erly be subjected to shoddy, slovenly, and trashy educational fare. College should be a demanding as well as an enriching experience—demanding for the brilliant youngster at a high level of expectation and for the less brilliant at a more modest level.

It is no sin to let average as well as brilliant youngsters into college. It *is* a sin to let any substantial portion of them— average or brilliant—drift through college without effort, with-out growth, and without a goal. That is the real scandal in many of our institutions.

We must expect students to strive for excellence in terms of the kind of excellence that is within their reach. Here we must recognize that there may be excellence or shoddiness in every line of human endeavor. We must learn to honor excel-lence in every socially accepted human activity, however hum-ble the activity, and to scorn shoddiness, however exalted the activity. An excellent plumber is infinitely more admirable than an incompetent philosopher. The society that scorns excellence in plumbing because plumbing is a humble activity and tolerates shoddiness in philosophy because it is an exalted activity will have neither good plumbing nor good philosophy. Neither its pipes nor its theories will hold water.

Opportunities Other than College

Not long ago the mother of two teen-age boys came to me for advice. "Roger made a fine record in high school," she explained, "and when he was a senior we had exciting discussions of all the colleges he was interested in. Now Bobby comes along with terrible grades, and when the question of his future arises a silence descends on the dinner table. It breaks my heart!"

I knew something about Bobby's scholastic limitations, which were notable, and I asked warily what I might do to help.

"The high-school principal says that with his record no college will take him," she said, "and that if one did take him he wouldn't last. I can't reconcile myself to that."

"Have you discussed any possibilities other than college?" I asked.

She shook her head. "His father says he can get him a job driving a delivery truck. But I think he just says that to jar Bobby."

It took some time for me to explain all that I thought was deplorable in her attitude and that of her husband. The young person who does not go on to college should be enabled to look forward to just as active a period of growth and learning in the post-high-school years as does the college youngster.

The nature of this continued learning will depend on the young person's interests and capacities.

Many young people who terminate their education short of college have had unrewarding experiences in the classroom and have a negative attitude toward anything labeled "learning" or "education." Even if they are not bitter about their school experiences, they are likely to feel that, having tried that path and failed, their salvation lies elsewhere. What they must be helped to recognize is that there are many kinds of further learning outside formal high-school and college programs. The fact that they have not succeeded in high school simply means that they must continue their learning in other kinds of situations.

Training programs within industrial corporations have expanded enormously and constitute a significant proportion of all education today. Apprenticeship systems are not as common as they used to be in the skilled crafts or trades, but they are still in operation in every major industry and offer opportunities for the ambitious youngster.

Some labor unions have impressive educational programs. The International Ladies Garment Workers Union, for example, offers a wide variety of opportunities.

Various branches of government offer jobs to high-school graduates that involve an opportunity to learn while working. The armed services offer training in many occupational specialties.

Night classes in the public schools are heavily attended, and much of present attendance is in trade courses for semiskilled or unskilled workers.

There also exist, in the amazingly variegated pattern of American education, many special schools—art schools, music schools, nursing schools, and the like—which should be considered by the young person not going on to college. The young people who wish to become oral hygienists or diesel mechanics or television repair specialists will find schools throughout the country at which they may receive training.

Correspondence study offers the most flexible opportunities for study beyond high school, but the young people who do not go on to college usually have little enthusiasm for paper-and-pencil work, and that is what correspondence study amounts to.

There are also educational opportunities on radio and television; and the possibilities of computer-assisted instruction are enormous.

Finally, jobs themselves are a form of education. In hard times, of course, young people take what jobs they can get. In better times, they should look at the array of jobs available not simply from the standpoint of money and convenience but from the standpoint of their own further growth. If young people are willing to think hard about their own abilities and interests, and then to look at available jobs as opportunities for self-development, they can look forward to years of learning and growth as rewarding as anything a college student might experience.

But we must make available to young people far more information than they now have on post-high-school opportunities other than college. Parents, teachers, and high-school counselors must recognize that if the youngster who is not going to college is to continue his growth and learning he must receive as much sagacious help and counsel as a college-bound student. As Ernest Boyer put it, "It is ironic that those who need the most help get the least."[2]

The paradox is this: exceptionally bright youngsters will

commonly have excellent counseling from their professors until their mid-twenties. Youngsters of limited ability, faced with far more baffling career problems, are likely to see their last counselor at age sixteen.

Michael Walzer argues that if the community subsidizes college education for exceptionally able youngsters, it should provide less able students with comparable subsidy for alternative forms of education.[3]

At the very least there should be in every school district, city, or county a counseling office prepared to offer educational and career advice to all out-of-school youngsters until they reach age twenty-one.

CHAPTER TWELVE

The Democratic Dilemma

The Paradox in Democracy

WE LIVE WITH a curious paradox. On the one hand, we love the idea of free and fair competition among individuals. We still have a long way to go in achieving our idea of equal opportunity, but it *is* our ideal. Nothing is dearer to our hearts than the notion that "anybody can be somebody," that youngsters who "have what it takes" can achieve success regardless of their beginnings—and, in theory at least, go as far as their ability and drive will take them.

But through our society generally rewards achievers without concern for their point of origin, it also gives the rest of us—all of us—ultimate control over the achievers, whatever their area of achievement may be. They may be brilliant politicians but we can refuse to vote for them. They may be high-powered salesmen but we can refuse to buy their product. They may set standards of excellence in art, music, or literature but we can choose to ignore those standards.

The freedom (and incentive) to achieve has good and bad results. On the good side it releases great human energies, fosters excellence in many fields of great value to the society, encourages problem solvers, and in general urges humans toward the peaks of performance. The bad side is that the "peaks of performance" are not invariably attractive. We have our champions of exploitation and our virtuosos of avarice.

The ultimate popular control also has good and bad results. It enables us to curb the exploiters and limit the abuse of power. The bad side is that it can inhibit excellence and stifle the person of superior gifts. It can permit the deterioration of standards, the debasement of taste, shoddy education, vulgar art, cheap politics, and the tyranny of the lowest common denominator,

> Where blind and naked Ignorance
> Delivers brawling judgments unashamed,
> On all things all day long.[1]

Institutional Defenses

A society that accepts performance as the chief determinant of status—as ours does—has great charm for those whose ability, drive, aggressiveness, or luck enables them to come out on top. It may have notably less charm for those who do not come out on top. The latter may be individuals of lesser ability or lesser motivation. They may have valid objections to the tactics of some of those who "come out on top." They may be individuals whose excellences are not of the sort that society at this particular moment chooses to reward. Or they may simply lack a temperament that takes kindly to the knife-edge of competition. There are many individuals of great gifts in the latter group.

For whatever reason, there are large numbers of individuals who will not necessarily find unrelieved exhilaration in a system that emphasizes high performance. If these large numbers come to believe that the system exposes them unnecessarily to frustration and defeat, and if they enjoy the freedom of social action characteristic of a democracy, they will create elaborate institutional defenses to diminish the emphasis on performance as a determinant of status. We can observe such institutional defenses not only in education but in every aspect of our national life.

Am I saying that our society is composed of a select layer of superior individuals who win, and a large mass of defensive losers who proceed to hobble them? Each winner a Gulliver pinned down by the Lilliputians? Not at all. Virtually every one of us participates in building the institutional defenses. No doubt there are piratical souls who would gladly hoist the black flag and operate outside all defense of an institutional nature. But most of us, including most of those who are winners in one or another dimension, want to set some reasonable limits.

Businesspeople provide the perfect example. They love to assert their devotion to competition, but they too are capable of powerful defensive action if competition becomes excessive. It is just such defensive action that Brandeis was referring to when he wrote, in 1912: " . . . the right of competition must be limited in order to preserve it. For excesses of competition lead to monopoly, as excesses of liberty lead to absolutism. . . . "[2] The top corporate executive is apt to be particularly eloquent in defense of individual competition, but his ambitious subordinates will usually find that he has himself well protected against any unseemly rivalry on their part.

Trade union practices are a veritable coral reef of accumulated defenses against extreme emphasis upon individual performance. One of the leading authorities on labor once said: "The good Lord made more slow workers than fast workers. Don't ask me why. The fast workers can look after themselves under any system. It is the business of the trade union to look after the slow ones." That is by no means the only task of the union, but the statement is correct.

One can discover in any Civil Service manual innumerable rules designed to blunt the edge of excessive emphasis on performance. Rules governing seniority and tenure, although they serve other important purposes, serve this purpose also.

The scholastic lockstep that was adopted in many of our schools, in which all youngsters are advanced a grade per year regardless of IQ and performance, was a means of preventing invidious comparisons among individuals. The underlying philosophy was vigorously stated by one educator in these terms: "Any school system in which one child may fail while another succeeds is unjust, undemocratic, and uneducational."[3]

In short, our society is full of institutional defenses against excessive emphasis on individual performance. Such defenses —in one form or another—will always be with us. They are often healthy reactions to excessive emphasis upon performance. But carried far enough these defenses too can constitute excesses and can diminish the concern for any standards whatsoever.

And in efforts to minimize differences in performance, we can detect not only the hand of the generous person who honestly regrets that some must lose the foot race but the hand of the envious ones who resent achievement, detest superiority in others, and will punish eminence at every opportunity. These latter are the ones Henri Becque had in mind when he said, "The defect of equality is that we only desire it with our superiors."[4]

Because of the leveling influences that are inevitable in popular government, a democracy must, more than any other form of society, maintain what Ralph Barton Perry has called "an express insistence upon quality and distinction." When it does not do so, the consequences are all too familiar. Standards are contagious. They spread throughout an organization or a society. If an organization or group cherishes high standards, the behavior of individuals who enter it is inevitably influenced. Similarly, if slovenliness infects a society, it is not easy for any member of that society to remain uninfluenced in his own behavior. With that grim fact in mind, one is bound to look with apprehension on many segments of our national life in which slovenliness has attacked like dry rot, eating away the solid timber.

The Rise of the Meritocracy

One way *not* to solve our problems is beautifully described in Michael Young's witty book entitled *The Rise of the Meritocracy* (1961).[5] Young's fictional account purports to be a description of the consequences in England between A.D. 1870 and 2033 of an ever-increasing emphasis upon sheer intelligence as a criterion for social advancement. At the beginning of this period, he points out, intelligence was widely distributed among all of the social classes. There were plenty of dull people whose upper-class status was assured by birth. And there were lots of bright people in the lower strata who had never had the opportunity to exhibit their ability.

He identifies the first move toward meritocracy as the introduction of the merit system into the Civil Service in 1870. After the great wars of the twentieth century forced nations to recognize that effective use of their human resources was necessary to survival, the search for talent proceeded apace. In Young's version of history, England rejected the idea of comprehensive schools as sentimental. Talented youngsters were sorted out early and given special treatment. In one after another segment of society, the merit principle replaced other methods of determining hierarchical relationships. One of the final triumphs came when the seniority principle was abolished, so that able individuals no matter how young could move instantly to the top if their ability warranted.

> . . . when casts were abolished . . . there was still another category of people to circumvent—the class of old men. . . . [Having] the wrong man in a position of power merely because he was of a superior age was every bit as wasteful as having the wrong man in a position of power merely because his parents were of a superior class.[6]

Eventually the whole society was pretty well sifted out. All the people at the top were very, very bright, all at the bottom were very, very dull. And since the less bright people (who of course far outnumbered the others) tended to elect parliamentary representatives in their own image, the House of Commons also declined in intelligence and power. The bright people went into the Civil Service, and it became the dominant factor in government.

Finally, some elements of the ruling classes suggested that since society had sorted itself out so that all the bright people were on top, one might as well return to the old heredity principle. It had been a bad principle, they admitted, at a time in history when many in the ruling class were stupid and many in the lower class were bright; but now, the argument ran, it would simply stabilize a healthy situation.

Despite the logic of it all, which the author sets out with great satirical skill, the system produced social tensions that resulted in uncontrollable riots.

The book is an amusing and effective sermon against a Utopia based upon rigorous and unimaginative application of the merit principle.

Where Does Wisdom Lie?

Fortunately, a thorough sorting out of the kind described by Michael Young will never occur. Thanks to assortative mating and the facts of genetics, both bright and dull children will continue to appear at every level of society. And the unpredictable factors of motivation, character, and personality will help defeat any neat sorting out of the kind he envisioned.

Even so, we have seen considerable movement in the direction he described, and we shall see more—more rigorous search for and selection of the ablest, more systematic placement of those so selected in high positions.

To the extent that this occurs it will evoke the institutional defenses described in the early pages of this chapter.

The issue is well exemplified in the problem we face with respect to gifted children. In the 1920s we went through a period of great interest in exceptionally able youngsters. But that period was succeeded by an almost savage rejection of any measures designed for the gifted youngster, and insistence on precisely the same treatment for all students.

Enthusiasm for the gifted youngster recurred rather briefly in the late 1950s after the Soviet Union orbited *Sputnik,* but faded swiftly in the climate of the sixties. In the early 1980s people were again willing to listen to recommendations for the education of the gifted—chiefly because they feared that the United States was losing the international competition in science and technology. But the basic problem has not changed. If the measures designed to assist the gifted youngster are such as to arouse hostility in those who are not gifted (and their parents), there is certain to be a backlash. Children who are not gifted—and parents who do not have gifted children—are in the great majority.

Those who care about excellence in education (and someone had *better* care!) must ask themselves how it is possible to cultivate it in ways that do not provoke such restraining or defeating countermoves.

I believe that an answer is to be found. But it requires first that we restate the problem in somewhat more constructive terms: How can we provide opportunities and rewards for individuals of every degree of ability so that individuals at every level will realize their full potentialities, perform at their best, and harbor no resentment toward those at any other level?

We have already touched upon some of the important ingredients of a solution. For example, seen in this context, our principle of multiple chances is not a sentimental compromise with efficient procedure but a measure well calculated to reduce the tensions to which our system is subject. The same may be said of the principle of avoiding labels that seem to identify some children as first-class citizens and others as second-class. And it is in this context that one may fully understand the virtues of the American comprehensive high school.

But vastly more important is to be clear in our minds about the pluralistic nature of excellence. Let us be insistent on the goal of excellence, but let us recognize that it takes many forms.

CHAPTER THIRTEEN

The Full Range of Human Excellence

The Many Kinds of Excellence

TO TALK REALISTICALLY ABOUT the environment for excellence in our society today, we must talk—as we have —of the search for talent, of schools and colleges, of testing procedures, and so on. But I have hinted here and there that those institutional considerations falsely narrow our view of the rich variety of human excellences. Let me now address the subject directly.

That there are many varieties of excellence is a truth of which we must continually remind ourselves. The Duke of Wellington, in a famous incident, revealed an enviable under-

standing of it. The government was considering the dispatch
of an expedition to Burma to take Rangoon. The Cabinet
summoned Wellington and asked him who would be the ablest
general to head such an undertaking. He said, "Send Lord
Combermere." The government officials protested: "But we
have always understood that Your Grace thought Lord Combermere a fool." The duke's response was vigorous and to the
point. "So he is a fool, and a damned fool, but he can take
Rangoon."[1]

In intellectual fields alone there are many kinds of excellence. There is the kind of intellectual activity that leads to a
new theory and the kind that leads to a new machine. There
is the mind that finds its most effective expression in teaching
and the mind that is most at home in research. There is the
mind that works best in quantitative terms and the mind that
luxuriates in poetic imagery.

There is excellence in art, in music, in craftsmanship, in
human relations, in technical work, in leadership, in parental
responsibilities. There are those who perform great deeds and
those who make it possible for others to perform great deeds.
There are pathfinders and path preservers. There are those who
nurture and those who inspire. There are those whose excellence involves doing something well and those whose excellence lies in being the kind of people they are, lies in their
kindness or honesty or courage.

There are kinds of excellence (e.g., athletics) in which a
scoreboard is essential and kinds of excellence so subjective
that the world cannot even observe much less appraise them.
Montaigne wrote, "It is not only for an exterior show or osten-
tation that our soul must play her part, but inwardly within
ourselves, where no eyes shine but ours."

There is a way of measuring excellence that involves comparison between people—some are musical geniuses and some are not; and there is another that involves comparison between myself at my best and myself at my worst. It is this latter comparison which enables me to assert that I am being true to the best that is in me—or forces me to confess that I am not.

Definitions of excellence tend to be most narrow at the point where we are selecting individuals, or testing them, or training them. In the course of daily life, mature people recognize many varieties of excellence in one another. But when we are selecting, testing, or training we arbitrarily narrow the range. The reasons for doing so are practical ones. To the extent that we admit a great variety of kinds of excellence we make the task of selection more difficult. Narrowing the grounds for selection is one way of making the selection process manageable—but as I have already pointed out in connection with testing, the narrowing may do a grave injustice to those whose dimensions of excellence fall outside the narrow range.

Consider the relatively narrow bottleneck through which most youngsters enter a career as a scientist. What they need to pass through that bottleneck is the capacity to manipulate abstract symbols and to give the kind of intellectual response required on intelligence or achievement tests. This capacity for abstract reasoning and for dealing with mathematical and verbal symbols is useful not only on the tests but in every course they take. There are other factors that contribute to success in graduate school, but most graduate students would agree that this is the heart and soul of the matter.

On the other hand, if one looks at a group of mature scientists—in their fifties, let us say—one finds that those who are respected have arrived at their high station by a remarkable variety of routes. A small proportion of the very bright ones have the special dimension of creativity that brings historic advances in their field. Others are honored for their extraordinary gifts as teachers: their students are their great contribution to the world. Others are respected—though perhaps not loved—for their devastating critical faculties. And so the list goes. Some are specialists by nature, some generalists; some creative, some plodding; some gifted in action, some in expression.

If we reflect on the way in which we judge our own contemporaries we will recognize the varied standards of judgment that come into play. But though, in daily life, we recognize a good many kinds of high performance, the range is still narrower than it should be. One way to make ourselves see this is to reflect on the diverse kinds of excellence that human beings have honored at different times and places. At any given time in a particular society, the idea of what constitutes excellence tends to be limited—but the conception changes as we move from one society to another or one century to another. Baltasar Gracián said: "It is not everyone that finds the age he deserves. . . . Some men have been worthy of a better century, for every species of good does not triumph. Things have their period; even excellences are subject to fashion."[2]

Taking the whole span of history and literature, the images of excellence are amply varied: Confucius teaching the feudal lords to govern wisely . . . Leonidas defending the pass at Thermopylae . . . Saint Francis preaching to the birds at Alviano . . . Lincoln writing the Second Inaugural "with malice toward none" . . . Mozart composing his first oratorio at the age of eleven . . . Kepler calculating the planetary orbits . . . Emily Dickinson jotting her "letters to the world" on scraps of paper . . . Jesus saying, "Father, forgive them; for they know not what they do." . . . Florence Nightingale nursing the wounded at Balaclava . . . Eli Whitney pioneering the manufacture of interchangeable parts . . . Ruth saying to Naomi, "Thy people shall be my people."

The list is long and the variety is great. Taken collectively, human societies have gone a long way toward exploring the full range of human excellences. But a particular society at a given moment in history is apt to honor only a portion of the full range. And wise indeed is the society that is not afraid to face hard questions about its own practices on this point. Is it honoring the excellences that are likely to be most fruitful for its own continued vitality? To what excellences is it relatively insensitive—and what does this imply for the tone and texture of its life? Is it squandering approbation on kinds of high performance that have nothing to contribute to its creativity as a society?

Those who can contemplate those questions without uneasiness have not thought very long nor very hard about excellence in the United States.

Toning up the Whole Society

A conception that embraces many kinds of excellence at many levels is the only one that fully accords with the richly varied potentialities of mankind; it is the only one that will permit high morale throughout the society.

Our society cannot achieve greatness unless individuals at many levels of ability accept the need for high standards of performance and strive to achieve those standards within the limits possible for them. We want the highest conceivable excellence, of course, in the activities crucial to our effectiveness and creativity as a society; but that isn't enough. We must foster a conception of excellence that may be applied to every degree of ability and to every socially acceptable activity. A plane may crash because the designer was incompetent or because the mechanic responsible for maintenance was incompetent. The same is true of everything else in our society. We need excellent physicists and excellent construction workers, excellent legislators and excellent first-grade teachers. The tone and fiber of our society depend upon a pervasive, almost universal striving for good performance.

And we are not going to get that kind of striving, that kind of alert and proud attention to performance, unless we can instruct the whole society in a conception of excellence that leaves room for everybody who is willing to strive—a conception of excellence which says that whoever I am or whatever I am doing, provided that I am engaged in a socially acceptable activity, some kind of excellence is within my reach. As James B. Conant put it, "Each honest calling, each walk of life, has its own elite, its own aristocracy based upon excellence of performance."

We cannot meet the challenges facing our society unless we can achieve and maintain a high level of morale and drive throughout the society. Men and women must have goals that, in their eyes, merit effort and commitment; and they must believe that their efforts will win them self-respect and the respect of others.

It is important to bear in mind that we are talking about an approach to excellence and a conception of excellence that will bring a whole society to the peak of performance. The gifted individual absorbed in his own problems of creativity and workmanship may wish to set himself narrow and very severe standards of excellence. The critic concerned with a particular development in art, let us say, may wish to impose a specialized criterion of excellence. This is understandable. But we are concerned with a broader objective.

This broader objective is critically important, even for those who have set themselves far loftier (and narrower) personal standards of excellence. We cannot have islands of excellence in a sea of slovenly indifference to standards. In an era when the masses of people were mute and powerless it may have been possible for a tiny minority to maintain high standards regardless of their surroundings. But today the masses of people are neither mute nor powerless. As consumers, as voters, as the source of public opinion, they heavily influence levels of taste and performance. They can create a climate supremely inimical to standards of any sort.

I am not saying that we can expect everyone to be excellent. It would please me if this were possible: I am not one of those who believe that a goal is somehow unworthy if everyone can achieve it. But those who achieve excellence will be few at best. All too many lack the qualities of mind or spirit that would allow them to conceive excellence as a goal, or to achieve it if they conceived it.

But many more can achieve it than now do. Many, many more can *try* to achieve it than now do. *And the society is bettered not only by those who achieve it but by those who are trying.*

The broad conception of excellence we have outlined must be built on two foundation stones—and both of them exist in our society.

—*A pluralistic approach to values.* American society has always leaned toward such pluralism. We need only be true to our deepest inclinations to honor the many facets and depths and dimensions of human experience and to seek the many kinds of excellence of which the human spirit is capable.

—*A universally honored philosophy of individual fulfill-ment.* We have such a philosophy, deeply embedded in our tradition. Whether we have given it the prominence it deserves is a question we must now examine.

CHAPTER FOURTEEN

Lifelong Learning and Growth

The Person One Could Be

IN OUR OWN SOCIETY one need not search far for an idea of great vitality and power that can and should serve the cause of excellence. It is the idea of lifelong learning and growth. The ideal is implicit in our convictions concerning individual fulfillment and the worth of the individual. I shall speak later of our obligations to the community, but for the moment let us focus on our belief that individuals should be enabled to achieve the best that is in them.

The most widely recognized formal means that we have devised to further that objective is the educational system. But education in the formal sense is only a part of the society's larger task of abetting the individual's intellectual, emotional, and moral growth. What we must reach for is a conception of perpetual self-discovery, perpetual reshaping to realize one's best self, to be the person one could be.

This is a conception that far exceeds formal education in scope. It includes not only the intellect but the emotions, character, and personality. It involves not only the surface but deeper layers of thought and action. It involves adaptability, creativeness, and vitality.

And it involves ethical and spiritual growth. We say that we wish the individual to fulfill his potentialities, but obviously we do not wish to develop great criminals or great rascals. Learning for learning's sake isn't enough. Thieves learn cunning, and slaves learn submissiveness. We may learn things that constrict our vision and warp our judgment. We wish to foster fulfillment within the framework of rational and moral strivings that have characterized humankind at its best. We respect men and women who place themselves at the service of values that transcend their own individuality—the values of their people, their heritage, their profession, and the religious and moral values that nourished the ideal of individual fulfillment in the first place. But this "gift of self" only wins our admiration if the giver has achieved a mature individuality and if the act of giving does not involve an irreparable crippling of that individuality. We cannot admire faceless, mindless servants of The State or The Cause or The Organization.

Waste on a Massive Scale

In our society today, large numbers of young people never fulfill their potentialities. Their environment may not stimulate such fulfillment, or it may actually stunt growth.

At a time when the nation must make the most of its human resources, it is unthinkable that we should resign ourselves to this waste of potentialities. Our strength, creativity, and growth as a society depend upon our capacity to develop the talents and potentialities of our people.

Any adequate attack on the problem will reach far beyond formal educational institutions. It will involve not only the school but the home, the church, the playground, and all other institutions that shape the individual. The Boy Scout or Girl Scout troop, the "Y," and hundreds of other volunteer groups must play their part—and play it more imaginatively than they have in the past.

Lifelong Learning

Commencement speakers are fond of saying that education is a lifelong process. And yet that is something that no young person with a grain of sense needs to be told. Why do the speakers go on saying it? It isn't that they love sentiments that are well worn with reverent handling (though they do). It isn't that they underestimate their audience. The truth is that they know something their young listeners do not know—something that can never be fully communicated. No matter how firm an intellectual grasp the young person may have on the idea that education is a lifelong process, he can never know it with the poignancy, with the deeply etched clarity, with the overtones of satisfaction and regret that an older person knows it. The young person has not yet made enough mistakes that cannot be repaired. He has not yet passed enough forks in the road that cannot be retraced.

The commencement speaker may give in to the temptation

to make it sound as though the learning experiences of his
generation were all deliberate and a triumph of character—
character that the younger generation somehow lacks. We can
forgive him that. It is not easy to tell young people how unpur-
posefully we learn, how life tosses us head over heels into our
most vivid learning experiences, how intensely we resist many
of the increments in our own growth.

But we cannot forgive him as readily if he leaves out another part of the story. And that part of the story is that the
process of learning through life is by no means continuous and
by no means universal. If it were, age and wisdom would be
perfectly correlated, and there would be no such thing as an
old fool. The sad truth is that for many of us the learning
process comes to an end very early indeed. And others learn the
wrong things.

We've all seen men and women, even ones in fortunate
circumstances with responsible positions, who seem to run out
of steam before they reach life's halfway mark. Perhaps life just
presented them with tougher problems than they could solve.
It happens. Perhaps something inflicted a major wound on
their confidence or their pride. Perhaps they were pulled down
by the hidden resentments and grievances that grow in adult
life, sometimes so luxuriantly that, like tangled vines, they
immobilize the victim.

It isn't a question of whether the individual gets to the peak
of the pyramid. We can't all get to the peak, and that isn't the
point of life anyway. The question is whether individuals, whatever their worldly success, have continued to learn and grow
and try.

The lessons of maturity are not learned, for the most part,
from books. We learn from our jobs. We learn from our friends
and families. We learn by accepting the commitments of life,

by playing the roles that life hands us, by getting older, by suffering, by taking risks, by loving, and by bearing life's indignities with dignity.

Nor are the things we learn in maturity simple things such as acquiring information and skills. We learn not to engage in self-destructive behavior. We learn not to burn up energy in anxiety. We learn to manage our tensions if we have any, which we do. We learn that self-pity and resentment are among the most toxic of drugs, and if we get addicted we break the habit at all costs.

We learn to bear with the things we can't change. We learn that most people are neither for us nor against us; they are thinking about themselves. We learn that no matter what we do, some people aren't going to love us—a lesson that is at first troubling and then quite relaxing.

There is an element of luck in personal development as in everything else, but Pasteur said that chance favors the prepared mind. And we all know individuals whose growth and learning can only be explained in terms of an inner drive, a curiosity, a seeking and exploring element in their personalities. Captain Cook said, "I . . . had ambition not only to go farther than any man had ever been before, but as far as it was possible for a man to go."[1] Just as Cook's restless seeking led him over the face of the earth, so others embark on odysseys of the mind and spirit.

Unfortunately, the conception of individual growth and lifelong learning that animates the commencement speaker finds no adequate reflection in our social institutions. For too long we have paid pious lip service to the idea and trifled with it in practice. Like those who confine their religion to Sunday and forget it the rest of the week, we have set "education" off in a separate category from the main business of life. It is

something that happens in schools and colleges to young people between the ages of six and twenty-one. It is not something
—we seem to believe—that need concern the rest of us.

But if we believe what we profess concerning the worth of
the individual, then the idea of individual development within
a framework of ethical purpose must become our deepest concern, our national preoccupation, our passion, our obsession.
We must think of education as relevant for everyone every-
where—at all ages and in all conditions of life.

What we are suggesting is that every institution in our
society should contribute to the growth of the individual. Every
institution must, of course, have its own purposes and preoccu-
pations, but over and above everything else that it does, it
should be prepared to answer the question posed by society:
What is your institution doing to foster the development of the
individual within it?

Now what does all of this mean? It means that we should
very greatly enlarge our ways of thinking about education. We
should be painting a vastly greater mural on a vastly more
spacious wall. What we are trying to do is nothing less than to
build a greater and more creative civilization. We propose that
the American people accept as a universal task the fostering of
individual development within a framework of rational and
ethical values—at every age, in every significant situation, in
every conceivable way.

If we accept this as an authentic national preoccupation,
the schools and colleges will then be the heart of a national
endeavor. They will be committed to the furthering of a national objective and not—as they now often find themselves—
swimming upstream against the interests of a public that thinks
everything else more urgent.

And both schools and colleges will be faced with a challenge beyond anything they have yet experienced. Above all they must gird the individual's mind and spirit for a never-ending process of growth. They cannot content themselves with the time-honored process of stuffing students like sausages or even the possibly more acceptable process of training them like seals. It is the obligation of the schools and colleges to instill in their students the attitudes toward growth, learning, and creativity that will in turn shape the society. With other institutions at work on other parts of this task, the schools and colleges must of course give particular attention to the intellectual aspects of growth. This is uniquely their responsibility.

If we accept without reservation the implications of our traditional belief in individual fulfillment, we shall have enshrined a highly significant purpose at the heart of our national life. We shall have accepted a commitment that promises pervasive consequences for our way of thinking about the purpose of democratic institutions. And we shall have embraced a philosophy that gives a rich personal meaning to the pursuit of excellence.

CHAPTER FIFTEEN

Talent and Leadership

U P TO THIS POINT our attention has been focused chiefly on individual excellence, but obviously there are kinds of excellence that characterize organizational endeavor. Indeed, much of our despair over mediocrity (and worse) on the contemporary scene is evoked by institutional failure—in our legislatures, government agencies, corporations, unions, professions, schools, and so on. All too often it seems that they not only fail to set standards of institutional excellence but inhibit the possibility of individual excellence.

It is with these considerations in mind that I turn to a consideration of leadership. I shall limit myself to certain aspects of the subject that are essential to this book.[1]

The Idea of a Natural Aristocracy

At the very beginning of our life as a nation, it was said that in our kind of society a "natural aristocracy" should arise to replace hereditary aristocracies. I doubt the usefulness of the concept but it merits discussion. Presumably the phrase denotes an open aristocracy whose ranks are replenished continuously by men and women of exceptional gifts. The idea was never more vividly expressed than by Thomas Jefferson, who had the opportunity to observe old-style aristocracy at its most corrupt.

> I hold it to be one of the distinguishing excellences of elective over hereditary successions, that the talents which nature has provided in sufficient proportion, should be selected by the society for the government of their affairs, rather than that this should be transmitted through the loins of knaves and fools, passing from the debauches of the table to those of the bed.[2]

But although this idea is appealing to Americans (or perhaps *because* it is appealing), it has never been subjected to hard critical examination.

Most academic people, if asked what the phrase ought to imply, would probably say "an aristocracy of intellect." As one academic friend of mine put it, "What other true aristocracy could there be?" But there are dissenting views that are legitimate and not anti-intellectual. Consider the words of Henry James, the elder.

> There are two very bad things in this American land of ours, the worship of money and the worship of intellect. Both money and intellect are regarded as good in themselves, and you consequently see the possessor of either eager to display his possessions to the public, and win the public recognition of the fact. But intellect is as essen-

tially *subordinate* a good as money is. It is good only as a minister and purveyor to right affections. . . .[3]

Many may disagree with James in some measure, but few will deny the grain of truth in what he says. Today we have vastly more reason to respect intellect, vastly more reason to be awed by the achievements of the human mind; but in our total scale of values it must still be a subordinate good. Our admiration for the person who puts extraordinary intellectual gifts at the service of chicanery is wry at best. We cannot admire intellectuals who lend themselves to the cause of tyranny and brutality. We admire scientists because they use their intellectual gifts in the service of one of the highest values of our civilization—the search for truth. We would not honor them if they used the same gifts for evil purposes.

In short, intellect alone is not sufficient basis for the creation of an aristocracy. There is no certainty that an aristocracy of intellect would be more virtuous, more humane, or more devoted to the dignity of the individual than the aristocracy of knaves and fools that repelled Thomas Jefferson.

Another objection to an aristocracy of the intellect might be entered by the many talented individuals whose gifts do not fall strictly within the meaning of the term "intellect." They might argue that the idea of an aristocracy of intellect is on the right track but too narrowly defined—that what we need is an *aristocracy of talent.*

But the criticism expressed by Henry James can be broadened too. There is nothing in the word "talent" that would lessen his concern. Indeed, he might well have quoted the comment of one of his contemporaries, H. F. Amiel: "Talent is glad enough, no doubt, to triumph in a good cause; but it easily becomes a freelance, content, whatever the cause, so long as victory follows its banner."[4]

Neither intellect nor talent alone can be the key to a position of leadership in our society. The additional requirement is a commitment to the highest values of the society.

Talent and Responsibility

In our society it is expected that power and responsibility will go hand in hand. We expect that those who have achieved influence in our society will conduct themselves with a commitment to the values that we hold in common and a sense of their obligation to the community. Our expectations are not always met, to put it mildly—and we are more tolerant of that outcome than we should be—but in the long run those who wield power irresponsibly are apt to be called to account.

Today many gifted individuals are enjoying a measure of influence they have never before experienced. To the extent that they do, they must demonstrate a lively devotion to the common good.

When gifted people speak of an aristocracy of talent, they rarely mention either responsibility or leadership. One gets the impression that they envisage a world in which talented people simply exercise their natural gifts and in consequence receive the rewards, the adulation and fealty that the term aristocracy implies—with none of the annoying burdens of leadership. The notion that they might have responsibilities beyond the skilled pursuit of their specialty or that they might exercise leadership (in the active and purposeful sense of that word) is often difficult for them to accept.

Historically, aristocracies have occasionally taken the view that their privileged position involved no obligations of leadership, but such aristocracies did not last long.

Thomas Jefferson was quite specific in outlining his own notion of the leadership functions of the natural aristocracy. In a letter to John Adams he said:

> The natural aristocracy I consider as the most precious gift of nature, for the instruction . . . and government of society. . . . May we not even say that that form of government is the best, which provides the most effectually for a pure selection of these natural *aristoi* into the offices of government?[5]

Similarly, when China, in the eighteenth and nineteenth centuries, was engaged in what was probably the most thorough effort ever made to select a governing class by examination, it was understood that the coveted membership in the gentry involved an obligation to exercise active leadership.[6]

Our Dispersed Leadership

The truth is that no matter how we modify or redefine it, the idea of a natural aristocracy remains a rather strained, romantic analogy. So let us drop the analogy and talk about our leadership on its own terms.

If we are to achieve excellence as a society, in our own way, true to our own style and distinctive characteristics, we are going to have to give attention to the quintessentially American system of leadership—and to deal as best we can with the flaws in that system.

We cannot hope to understand the nature of leadership in this country unless we shift attention from the rarefied upper strata and look at all the various levels and kinds of leaders that it requires to keep this nation functioning in a vital way (and to encourage excellence throughout the society).

Our imagination has been seized by the larger-than-life, charismatic leader who towers above his contemporaries, enjoys extraordinary personal renown, and leads in the grand style. But our preoccupation with the "storybook" leader may block our recognition of the other forms of leadership that exist in our society and constitute the only means we have for dealing effectively with the multiple interlocking systems and turf-protecting constituencies that characterize contemporary social organization.

I recall a conversation with Dwight Eisenhower not long after World War II in which he emphasized the importance to military effectiveness of leaders at every level all the way down the line. Indeed, he insisted that the most critical element in the leadership of troops is the noncommissioned officer.

It's interesting that military people, whom we think of as being unduly impressed by the high brass, are generally well aware of the point Eisenhower was making, whereas we civilians, who think we are duly skeptical of top leaders, are in fact fascinated by them and almost never think about the "down-the-line" leaders who exist in civilian life.

We may not think about them, but the country couldn't function without them. Leadership in our society is dispersed to an extraordinary degree. Despite the lavish media attention to high-level leaders, we are not wholly dependent on leadership at the top. We are dependent on leaders who function at many levels and in all segments of our society—business, government, organized labor, agriculture, the professions, the minority communities, the arts, the universities, social agencies, and so on. They are city councilmen and school superintendents, factory managers and editors, heads of local unions and heads of social agencies, lawyers and health commissioners.

If it weren't for this wide dispersal of leadership, our kind
of society couldn't function. Excessive dependence on central
definition and rule making produces standardized solutions to
be applied uniformly throughout the system. But the world
"out there," the world to be coped with, isn't standardized. It
is diverse, localized, and surprising.

Our top leaders have a crucial role in helping us to achieve
a sense of direction, to aid us in sifting priorities and clarifying
values. But the old, hierarchical model is of limited value today.
Less and less can top leaders, political, corporate, or whatever,
make the system work without the help of many others
throughout the society or organization. When we refer to "our
system," we obscure the fact that the nation is made up of
innumerable subsystems loosely related in ever-changing config-
urations—subsystems that sometimes mesh but often clash.
The difficult task of making fluid, interacting systems function
effectively cannot be ordained in Washington nor for that
matter in the headquarters of a corporation. A great many
capable people in various segments of the system must take the
initiative in responsible action to improve the functioning of
the system at their level, reweaving connections between warring subsystems and proposing redesign of malfunctioning processes.

There is continuous dialogue up and down the scale among
the various levels of leadership, and those below have a good
deal to do with what goes on above. Not only lower-level
leaders but rank-and-file followers may invite good or bad leadership at higher levels. And it is no doubt true that we generally
get the leadership we deserve. Good constituents tend to produce good leaders.

It sounds incredibly complicated. But despite the complications, our system of dispersed leadership is in fact flourishing. It has serious problems, and it could be vastly improved. But, as it has evolved, it is an extraordinary system. And, extraordinary or not, it is the system that exists. If we are to achieve excellence in any aspect of our functioning as a society, it will be within the context of this system.

What about the quality of the leaders up and down the line? Deploring the quality of our leadership is a firmly rooted tradition, like students deploring the food in the school cafeteria; and I'm sure the reader would welcome a confirmation of the tradition. But scanning the course of history and the diverse societies of today's world, one is bound to conclude that we are among the more fortunate in the human quality of our dignitaries up and down the line.

We could do better—and I've picked up a few bruises in the struggle to ensure that we do better. But that's a long story. Let us confine ourselves to certain critical aspects of our leadership system that bear on the capacity of our society to achieve excellence.

The War of the Parts against the Whole

One problem is that a high proportion of leaders in all segments and at all levels of our society today—business, labor, the professions, and so on—are rewarded for singleminded pursuit of the interests of their group regardless of the damage it may do the common good.

Obviously, a society of dispersed power and initiative will be characterized by pluralism, meaning by pluralism a philosophy and set of social arrangements that permit the existence of many competing ideas, many belief systems, many competing economic units. We like that. But pluralism is one thing and divisiveness is another. Our divisiveness in this society today approaches incoherence.

An example of our divisiveness may be seen in our reaction when outsiders offer gloomy appraisals of our condition as a nation. Observers have warned us in the strongest possible terms that we are endangering our future by our self-indulgence and our lack of commitment. And how are those stern warnings received? In one ear and out the other.

Why? Because everyone who hears them agrees but thinks the warnings apply to some other group of Americans. Not to *me*. Not to *my* group. Not to *my* kind of American.

Unfortunately, the warnings apply to all of us. If we can't face that fact we're lost.

We are strong believers in pluralism. But one worries about a society in which each constituent part blames the others and all scramble greedily for their own advantage, without any regard for the republic they profess to love. They have every right to be out there scrambling. But for them to ignore utterly, at times undermine, our shared concerns as a nation—that's not smart. They cannot forever deceive themselves that the common enterprise needs no attention from them. As A. E. Housman said, "The house of delusions is cheap to build but drafty to live in."

A pluralism that is not undergirded by some shared values, that reflects no commitment whatever to the commonweal, is pluralism gone berserk.

Our pluralistic philosophy invites each organization, institution, or special group to develop its own potentialities. But the price of that treasured autonomy and self-preoccupation is that each institution also concern itself with the common good. That is not idealism; it is self-preservation. If the larger system fails, the subsystems fail. If the nation fails we all fail. The war of the parts against the whole is a hazardous undertaking.

The fragmentation that afflicts us is not a characteristic of our system that people like to think about. The myth of a coherent establishment and the hardy vigor of conspiracy theories stem from our wanting to believe that *someone* is minding the store. But our society is not manipulated by a few powerful people behind the scenes. I've been behind the scenes and it's so crowded you can hardly move around. It's like Times Square on New Year's Eve.

This is a moment when the innumerable interests, organizations, and groups that make up our national life must keep their part of the bargain with the society that gives them freedom by working toward the common good. At least for now, a little less *pluribus,* a lot more *unum.*

Today our leaders in all segments and at all levels of our society work more or less exclusively for the good of their own segment. That's what we expect of them. But suppose the expectations changed. Suppose we made it customary to ask some uncomfortable questions of the men and women who have achieved prominence in the organizations and institutions that make up the society: Are they One-Segment Leaders, insulated from other parts of the community? Do they fatten on the deference of their own little circle, without ever seeking to understand the other worlds that make up their society? Or do they make an effort to reach out across boundaries, communicate with other segments, and seek to develop shared goals?

I have a friend who says that unless we have strong communities we shall always be ruled by distant masters. He loves the idea of community. The only trouble is he can't stand the people at the other end of town. We have to do better than that.

The first duty of our dispersed leaders is to establish communication among the highly organized (and often warring) segments of our society—business, labor, farmers, professional groups, and so on—to reweave the social fabric. Each segment must find a way of flourishing that is compatible with, even contributes to, the flourishing of other segments and the well-being of the whole society.

We must develop networks of leaders who accept some measure of responsibility for the society's shared concerns. Call them *networks of responsibility*, leaders of disparate or conflicting interests who undertake to act together in behalf of the shared concerns of the community or nation. Such networks will not flourish in the contemporary climate if they resemble the old Establishments in being exclusionary. Access and openness to participation must be their hallmark.

We had better admit that we have been witnessing the collapse of communities of obligation and commitment. We have learned that the fiercely destructive currents of modern life can undermine the authority of human institutions and frameworks of law and custom with deadly swiftness. The rebuilding is not so swift. A human community is the child of time.

The rebuilding of our communities—and our sense of community—is a natural job for our dispersed leaders. But for most of them that goal doesn't seem very important. One recalls the man who declined to contribute to his church because of his heavy debts. His minister said, "Surely you owe more to God than to anyone else"; and he said, "Yes, but God isn't pressing me." Leaders of the various fragmented interests feel much the same about the goal of rebuilding community—worthy but not pressing.

But in a system in which responsibility is not concentrated

at the center, every one had better be partly responsible. So it is for a community, so it is for the nation—and, most poignantly, so it is for the only livable planet we know about.

We need, at community, national, and international levels, leaders skilled in relating their own constituencies to others, and skilled in the arts of conflict resolution.

CHAPTER SIXTEEN

Leadership and Motivation

Large-Scale Organization

ANOTHER VITAL TASK facing our many levels of leadership is that of building motivation and morale—and the shared values that underlie them. Without motivation and morale, we are unlikely to achieve excellence as a society or to provide the environment in which individual excellence can occur.

The task is made more difficult by some of the familiar ailments of large-scale organization—a sense of powerlessness on the part of the individual, loss of a sense of identity, and so on. For most of this century we have moved steadily toward a society dominated by large-scale organization—huge governmental bureaucracies, huge corporations, huge unions. It's understandable. We had big goals—industrially, governmentally, socially—that required large-scale organization. But we were slow to reckon the cost—in the dimming of initiative, the deadening of creativity, and the sheer frustration to the individual of being caught up in vast, impersonal systems.

A friend of mine says, "What depresses me is that everything has gotten so big it's not only incomprehensible but unworkable. The huge government agencies can't even govern themselves. The great corporations can't begin to comprehend the vast economic networks in which they live."

The ailments of large-scale governmental bureaucracies have been assailed by critics for years. And when I think—to use Justice Holmes's phrase—of the little fragments of my fleece that I've left on the hedges of life, I sometimes think of my dealings with that particular world.

In contrast to governmental bureaucracies, the growth of huge corporate bureaucracies has received far less searching criticism over the years. Alfred Sloan was one of those who saw the problem early, and he warned long ago that as corporations increase in size and complexity, thought must be given to dispersing leadership and management functions throughout the system. But aside from Sloan, Robert Wood, Chester Barnard, and a few others, there weren't many critical voices raised as the corporations drifted into the swamp of large-scale organization.

All of that is changed now, of course, and the corporate world is taking the lead in new approaches to the problem. Linus (in the "Peanuts" cartoon) once said that there's no problem so big and complicated that it can't be run away from. He's wrong on this one. We can't run away from large-scale organization. But many corporate leaders now agree that it is necessary and possible to redesign our large-scale systems in such a way that they release energy rather than smother it, motivate rather than deaden, invite individual initiative rather than apathy. Corporate leaders are asking themselves how they can travel the road back from huge central staffs, excessively complex organizational charts, units too big to be manageable, and a morale-destroying impersonality, how they can push initiative downward and outward through the organization and encourage individual responsibility and identification with shared goals.

As Thomas J. Peters and Robert H. Waterman pointed out in their lively book *In Search of Excellence,* [1] the corporations that have dealt most effectively with these problems have gained a new appreciation of their own many-leveled leadership, right down to the shop foreman and the deputy section chief. They have discovered that these first-level, front-line leaders can accomplish things the head office can't equal—in raising productivity, in quality control, in sustaining morale.

It will be a great thing for our society if corporate leaders come to realize that what they are discovering with respect to their own organizations is equally true for the society as a whole. In the nation, as in large corporations, leaders at many levels and in all segments of the society must take the initiative in responsible action to improve the functioning of the system at their level. And they will not take that kind of initiative unless they believe they have a piece of the action.

The fact that corporate leaders have awakened to the problems of maintaining morale and vitality in large-scale organization is beginning to penetrate the consciousness of old-line government administrators. Government agencies have the same task industry does of revitalizing their own employees, but they must also learn new ways of dealing with leaders in

state and local government and in profit and nonprofit segments of the private sector, ways of dealing that preserve the
initiative and autonomy of the nonfederal partner.

Motives, Values, Vision

Quite aside from the problems of large-scale organization,
leaders, whether they are factory managers, hospital administrators, or municipal bureau chiefs, can never escape the problem of motivation.

It's a mistake to suppose that Americans have lost the
capacity for highly motivated action. But to evoke it, we are
going to have to get back on familiar terms with the things that
move people to inspired action.

Leaders don't invent motivation in their followers, they
unlock it. They work with what is there. Of course, "what is
there" is generally a great tangle of motives. Leaders tap those
that serve the purposes of group action in pursuit of shared
goals.

One could argue that such capacity to motivate others is a
quality to be expected of only the most exceptional human
beings. Nonsense. Anyone with a reasonably broad acquaintance can point to an athletic coach or elementary school teacher
or head of a sales force who is an excellent natural motivator.
The gift is rare but not exceedingly so, and in fields such as those
mentioned it is pulled to the surface quickly because the returns
from high motivation are so promptly apparent. In other fields
the effect of high or low motivation may be masked and the
leaders in those fields may ignore it—to their loss. In addition,
we have all become so sophisticated that the task of motivating
may seem somewhat juvenile anyway. You're asking me in my
pin-stripe suit to act like an athletic coach?

So organizations die of sophistication and more vibrant organizations replace them. Someone must see to maintenance of the morale necessary to undertake arduous endeavors. Someone has to call for the kind of effort and restraint, drive and discipline that make for great performance. Someone has to nurture a workable level of unity.

Such leaders must understand the wants and purposes and values of their people, and they must know how to overcome the inertia that afflicts most people most of the time. In this process, shared values are crucial.

But the contemporary world is destructive of shared values. It disintegrates families and communities, which are the ground-level generators of values. A central challenge to leadership at all levels is to counter such trends. We must reexamine our shared values and renew them. We must embed them in our institutions and not permit them to float off into a disembodied existence in sermons and commencement speeches. And we have to recognize that the regeneration of values is an endless task. Each generation draws from its inherited tradition those values that give strength and continuity to its common life—and reinterprets them for contemporary application.

Leaders assert a vision of what the society (or community or organization) can be at its best. They teach the framework of values. It didn't stop with Moses. Jefferson, Gandhi, Churchill, and many others come to mind. Of course, teaching the value framework can be overdone. Thomas Reed, who was Speaker of the House in the 1890s, once said to President Theodore Roosevelt, "Mr. President, if there's one thing I admire about you more than any other it's your original discovery of the Ten Commandments."

It is essential to a society's health—obviously—that people have confidence in their institutions. But they don't need to believe that their society is perfect. Far from it. They need to believe that on balance it is likely to meet their basic needs and confirm their values—*or that it is moving toward* meeting needs and confirming values. Humans have always lived partly on present satisfaction, partly on hope. And it's the task of the leader to keep hope alive. It is the ultimate fuel.

Psychologists have ways of measuring what individuals think is possible as a result of their own intentional behavior. Attitudes range from total fatalism ("Everything is determined by forces outside myself") to total confidence in one's own control of events. It should come as no surprise to learn that individuals from impoverished populations tend to be bunched at the fatalistic end of the scale; and unfortunately the lack of belief that any act of theirs will better their lives leads all too often to a deadening passivity.

I was talking once with a farmhead in Venezuela who was working on a rather promising experimental farm, and I asked him if he thought the experiment would prove beneficial. He said, "I think maybe it will benefit somebody, but it will not benefit me or my people. For us, nothing ever changes."

One must pause to reflect on the depth of subjugation reflected in that remark. The final stage of subjugation is the extinction of hope. The oppression experienced by those who fear machine guns and manacles is shallow compared to the oppression suffered by those who, over generations, are finally completely subjugated by their own lack of hope.

I cite the extreme case to dramatize the point, but the problem in more moderate forms is known to every teacher and leader.

In 1967 I had a conversation with Martin Luther King, Jr., at an educational conference. A black woman had just presented a paper entitled, if I remember correctly, "First, Teach

Them To Read." King leaned over to me and said, "First, teach them to believe in themselves." Strictly speaking, of course, she could teach them to believe in themselves while teaching them to read. But King was making an important point. Any leader, any athletic coach, any teacher, any counselor, understands.

Creativity within an organization or society is to be found among men and women who are far removed from the fatalistic end of the scale. They have a powerful conviction that they can affect events *in some measure*. Leaders at every level must help their people keep that belief. There are all too many factors in contemporary life that diminish it.

An obstacle to sound motivation and morale is the Utopianism which says that humans and their societies are perfectible, that we can, if we're smart, figure out the perfect state of things and achieve it. Then we can all relax. Life in a hammock. People who hold that view are then very disappointed when we don't achieve the perfect state of things. They tried hard, they were bright, and their intentions were good—and yet problems remain. Is there no rest for the weary? As a matter of fact, there isn't. It's an endless struggle, and humans, contrary to popular myth, are well fitted for that endless struggle.

Challenge and Response

Good teachers and good leaders share a bit of knowledge that is not universally recognized. They know that if they expect a lot of their respective constituencies, they increase the likelihood of high performance. A teacher of handicapped children said to me, "It's a sin to ask too little of these children. If we ask too little of them, they'll ask too little of themselves.

They have to ask a lot of themselves."

"Expect a lot, get a lot." That means standards, an explicit regard for excellence. In a high-morale society, people expect a lot of one another, hold one another to high standards. And leaders play a special role in conveying such expectations. Good leaders don't ask more than their constituents can give, but they often ask—and get—more than their constituents intended to give or thought it was possible to give.

Every emergency, every crisis reveals unsuspected resources of personal strength in some people and evokes heightened motivation in almost all. In speaking of the hero born of such a crisis, people say, "I didn't know he had it in him." But most of us have, in fact, a better, stouter-hearted, more vigorous self within us—a self that's deliberately a little hard of hearing but by no means stone deaf.

We all know that some organizations, some families, some athletic teams, some political groups inspire their members to great heights of personal performances. In other words, high individual performance will depend to some extent on the capacity of the society or institution to evoke it.

When an institution, organization, or nation loses its capacity to inspire high individual performance, its great days are over.

We are beginning to understand that the various kinds of talents that flower in any society are the kinds that are valued in the society. On a visit to Holland, my wife asked our hostess why children and adults in that country showed such an extraordinarily high incidence of language skills. "We expect it of children," the woman said simply. "We think it important." High performance takes place in a framework of expectation.

The fact has implications far beyond education. It means that, as a society, we shall have only the kinds of talent we

nourish, only the kinds of talent we want and expect. *Are we
nourishing the kinds of talent that will create a great civilization?* In matters relating to talent and society that is not just
another question. It is The Question.

One difficulty is that we shall get more or less precisely
what we deserve. We cannot worship frivolity and expect our
young people to scorn it. We cannot scorn the life of the mind
and expect our young people to honor it. H. W. Shaw said, "To
bring up a child in the way he should go, travel that way
yourself once in a while."[2] Our children will respect learning
if their elders respect learning. They will value the things of the
mind and spirit if the society values them.

But though the child is indirectly influenced by these
broader attitudes in the society as a whole, his growth depends
more directly on the character of his own immediate world—
his family and neighborhood. If this small world has the power
to nourish and challenge his mind and spirit, the shortcomings
of the larger society matter little. Thus in an earlier generation,
even in the bleakest frontier community a youngster might be
inspired to a lifetime of learning by parents who cared about
his education.

For adults, leaders have a major responsibility in establishing the framework of expectation.

Expectation and Faith

Let me broaden the point and express it in another way.
Good leaders and good teachers, as our culture measures good-
ness in those callings, must have a positive view of what can
be accomplished.

Obviously optimism can be carried to the point of foolish-
ness. Someone has said that pessimists got that way by financ-

ing optimists. Churchill was a master at building the British people's confidence in themselves, but he understood that optimism must be tempered with realism. He said, "I have nothing to offer but blood, toil, tears and sweat." In truth, he had a great deal more to offer, but he was saying, as all great leaders must, that it wasn't going to be easy. And he was saying what all leaders sooner or later find themselves saying—that failure is simply a reason to strengthen resolve.

But much of human performance is conditioned by what the performer thinks is possible for him. Leaders understand that. There was a time when people thought it was physically impossible to run a four-minute mile. When Roger Bannister ran it in under four minutes, he broke the physical barrier and the mental barrier as well. Two other runners accomplished the feat in a matter of weeks.

William James said, "Just as our courage is often a reflex of someone else's courage, so our faith is often a faith in someone else's faith." If you believe in me, it's easier for me to believe in myself.

In leading, in teaching, in dealing with young people, in all relationships of influencing, directing, guiding, helping, nurturing, the whole tone of the relationship will be conditioned by our faith in human possibilities. That is the generative element, the source of the current that runs beneath the surface of such relationships.

To conclude this discussion, I ask readers to renew their acquaintance with a leader who understood all of these considerations out of the depths of his own being. I urge readers, on their next visit to Washington, to find their way down to the western end of the Mall and revisit the Lincoln Memorial. It will be essential, of course, to take some time to study the face of Lincoln. Few images are more deeply etched in our minds and memories—and in a nation virtually without icons, few images are so closely associated with our sense of ourselves as a people.

He is the president who touched our souls. On the one hand he was the homespun, rather awkward man who said, "I have endured a great deal of ridicule without much malice, and have received a great deal of kindness not quite free from ridicule," and on the other hand he was the great leader-teacher whose heart-piercing words are inscribed on the north and south walls of the Memorial. I won't quote them here. Go read them.

To select, not at random, one of Lincoln's great qualities, he had faith in the people of this country. In the conventional model, people want to know whether the followers believe in the leader. I want to know whether the leader believes in the followers.

If our leaders at all levels are to be capable of lifting us and moving us toward excellence, they are going to have to believe in the people of this nation—a people able to perform splendidly and inclined to perform indifferently, a people deeply troubled in their efforts to find a future worthy of their past, a people capable of greatness and desperately in need of encouragement to achieve that greatness.

CHAPTER SEVENTEEN

The Aims of a Free People

Freedom and Obligation, Liberty and Duty

MORE THAN two centuries ago the founders of this nation set out to show the world that free citizens could build a great civilization. They knew that the world was watching them and they had sublime confidence that they were going to show the world something worth watching. Today you may survey vast stretches of contemporary life without detecting any sign that Americans remember that high goal. Our founders knew that in a world largely hostile to the idea of freedom, as the world was then and is now, a free society would have to prove that it is capable of—and worthy of—survival. The requirement is unchanged today. Free societies must prove their ability to make good on their promises and to keep alive their cherished values. And more than that, they must prove their vigor, their capacity to practice the disciplined virtues, their capacity to achieve excellence.

The free society is still the exceptional society: the ideal is still unattainable or unacceptable to most of the world's peoples. Many live under governments that have no inclination to foster freedom. Others are hemmed in by their own backwardness, or by rigid social stratification. The foes of freedom are still ready to argue that the unruliness, greed, and self-indulgence of human beings make a free society simply impractical.

It is hard for Americans to realize that the survival of the idea for which this nation stands is not inevitable. It may survive if enough Americans care enough. Part of the problem is that many individuals today no longer have a compelling feeling for the mutual dependence of the individual and the group, meaning by group the family, community, and nation.

The family and community have much to give the individual: nurture in infancy, the release of potentialities through education, the protection of individual rights, a sense of identity and belonging. In return, the individual must pay tithes of allegiance—must give something back—to family, community, nation, humankind.

We're free within a framework of obligations to our family, to our community, to the nation—and, of course, depending upon our beliefs, obligations to our God and to our conception of an ethical order.

We must freely grant our allegiance to the society that gives us freedom. Montesquieu said a republic can survive only as long as its citizens love it. Freedom and obligation, liberty and duty—that's the deal. May we never forget it. May we never deceive ourselves. It isn't in the grand design that we can have freedom without obligation. Not for long.

Reaffirmation

I believe that most Americans would welcome a new burst of commitment. I do not believe the self-centeredness and disengagement of which they are accused is their natural state. *The best kept secret in America today is that people would rather work hard for something they believe in than live a life of aimless diversion.*

Ask retired persons whether they would trade their leisure for activity in which they could apply their full powers toward something they believed in. The religious precept that you must lose yourself to find yourself is no less true at the secular level. No one who has observed devoted scientists in their laboratories can doubt the spiritual rewards of such work. The same is true of all who are working toward goals that represent the highest values of their society.

Of course, we all have a certain skepticism about the expenditure of effort beyond that required by the exigencies of the system. What's in it for me? It is a question born of deep habituation to the marketing of one's energies in return for the necessities of life. But we are talking now about another kind of arena and another kind of transaction. And this transaction is not subject to the same peasant craftiness. Quite the reverse. The more one gives, the more one gets.

We fall into the error of thinking that happiness necessarily involves ease, diversion, tranquillity—a state in which all of one's wishes are satisfied. For most people, happiness is not to be found in this vegetative state but in striving toward meaningful goals. For dedicated men and women life is the endless pursuit of goals, some of them unattainable. Such people may often be tense, worried, fatigued. They may have little of the leisure one associates with the storybook conception of happiness.

But the truth is that happiness in the sense of total gratification is not a state to which humans can aspire. It is for the cows, possibly for the birds, but not for us.

Of course, every line of behavior has its pathology, and there is a pathology of dedication. People sometimes commit themselves to vicious goals; or their commitment to worthy goals becomes so fanatical that they destroy as much as they create. And there is the "true believer" who surrenders himself to a mass movement or to dogmatic beliefs to escape the responsibilities of freedom. But a free society wants only one kind of devotion, the devotion of free, rational, responsible individuals.

Shared Purposes

A free people, precisely because they prize individuality, must take special pains to insure that their shared purposes do not disintegrate. No society will successfully resolve its internal conflicts if its only asset is cleverness in the management of these conflicts. It must also have compelling goals that are shared by the conflicting parties; and it must have a sense of movement toward these goals. The conflicting elements must have a vision that lifts their minds and spirits above the tensions of the moment.

It is not entirely easy to suggest a list of aims on which Americans would agree; but that is as it should be. We do not want or expect Americans to come to full agreement on a standard list of goals. We expect individual Americans to set their own priorities, not only in their personal lives but in matters affecting the common good. The result is diversity of values, diversity of opinion, diversity of aims. But most Americans are not really in doubt about the more serious of our

shared aims. *We know what they are. We know that they are difficult. And we know that we have not achieved them.*
Are examples needed?

We want peace with justice. We want a world that doesn't live in fear of the bomb, a world that acknowledges the rule of law, a world in which no nation can play bully and no nation need live in fear. How many Americans would disagree with that purpose? Is it easy? Have we achieved it? Read your morning paper.

We want freedom. We don't think the individual was born to have someone else's foot on his neck—or someone else's hand over his mouth. We want freedom at home and we want a world in which freedom is possible. Who would disagree with that as a national aim? Who would call it easy? Who would say we've achieved it?

We believe in the dignity and worth of the individual and it is our unshakable purpose to protect and preserve that dignity.

We believe that men and women should be enabled to achieve the best that is in them, and we are the declared enemies of all conditions, such as disease, ignorance, or poverty, that stunt the individual and prevent such fulfillment.

We believe in equality of all our citizens, regardless of race, gender, or religion, with respect to the rights specified in the Constitution.

Will there be arguments as to *how* to achieve these goals? Of course. Are there dissidents who don't believe in one or another of these goals—or any of them for that matter? Of course.

These items do not exhaust the list. But they are enough to demonstrate the possibility of formulating aims on which large numbers of Americans can agree.

A list of national purposes cannot—and should not—include all of the things that individuals in the society cherish. Our kind of society gives ample scope to aims that are essentially individual in nature—such as devotion to loved ones, and religious purposes.

Although we have been talking about the secular aims of the society, most of these aims have roots in our religious tradition. The religious substratum in American life runs deep and has marked us indelibly as a people. Some of the aims we have listed were conceived and brought to flower in a religious tradition. Others, though not religious in origin, have drawn powerful nourishment from religious groups and individuals. To state the matter in general terms, there is bound to be an intimate connection between the individual's attitude toward these aims and those deeper dealings with "the universal and eternal" that we call religion.

We Need Our Young People

Perhaps nothing is more effective in suppressing any spirit of public endeavor on the part of the individual than the overpowering size and complexity of the joint enterprise in which we are supposed to be participants. The tasks facing our ancestors may have been grim and often frightening, but generally they were also obvious. Each person knew what he or she must do. But what does the individual do about inflation, about international organization, about the balance of trade? Individual Americans—busy earning a living, repapering the dining room, getting the children off to school, and paying the bills —don't hear one clear call to action. They hear a jumble of outcries and alarms, of fanfares and dirges, of voices crying

"Hurry!" and voices crying "Wait!" Meanwhile they have problems of their own.

If it is confusing to adults, it is even more so for young people. How can they believe that they are even needed? Surely only great organizations can cope with such a giant system. If there is a problem, surely highly coordinated teams of experts must be studying it. If there are cracks in the world, learned specialists must be measuring them.

In short, complexity seems to be the universal condition, organization the universal requirement. What can the individual do? It is not surprising that young people shrug their shoulders and find something else to talk about.

This is disturbing when one recognizes the exhilarating effect of being needed and responding to that need—whether the need is within one's family, one's community, one's nation, or humankind. There is danger in a conviction on the part of young people that they are not needed by their own community. "The sense of uselessness," said Thomas Huxley, "is the severest shock which our system can sustain."[1]

But we do need our young people—desperately. Why not tell them we need every bit of help we can get? As Whitehead said, "We must produce a great age, or see the collapse of the upward striving of our race."[2]

One thing we might tell them—at the same time that we're telling ourselves—is this: "If you believe in a free society, be worthy of a free society." Every good man or woman strengthens society. In this day of sophisticated judgments on such matters, that is a notably unfashionable thing to say, but it is true. Men and women of integrity, by their very existence, rekindle the belief that as a people we can live above the level of moral squalor. We need that belief; a cynical community is a corrupt community.

More than any other form of government, democracy requires a certain faith in human possibilities. The best argument
for democracy is the existence of men and women who justify
that faith. It follows that one of the best ways to serve democracy is to be that kind of person.

The Pursuit of Excellence

When we raise our sights, strive for excellence, dedicate
ourselves to the highest goals of our society, we are enrolling
in an ancient and meaningful cause—the age-long struggle of
humans to realize the best that is in them. Humans reaching
toward the most exalted goals they can conceive, striving impa-
tiently and restlessly for excellence, have achieved religious
insights, created works of art, penetrated secrets of the universe
and set standards of conduct that heighten our sense of pride
—and dignity as human beings. William Hazlitt said, "Man is
the only animal that laughs and weeps; for he is the only animal
that is struck with the difference between what things are and
what they ought to be."[3] On the other hand, humans without
standards, with their eyes on the ground, have proved over and
over again, in every society, and at every period of history—
including the present—that they can be lower than the beasts,
morally and ethically blind, living a life devoid of meaning. A
concern for excellence, a devotion to standards, a respect for
the human mind and spirit at its best move us toward the
former condition and away from the latter. C.G.J. Jacobi,
when asked why he devoted himself to mathematics, said,
"Pour l'honneur de l'esprit humain."

William James said: "Democracy is on trial, and no one
knows how it will stand the ordeal. . . . What its critics now

affirm is that its preferences are inveterately for the inferior. So it was in the beginning, they say, and so it will be world without end. Vulgarity enthroned and institutionalized, elbowing everything superior from the highway, this, they tell us, is our irremediable destiny. . . ."[4]

William James himself did not believe that this was our destiny. Nor do I. But let us not deceive ourselves. The specter that William James raised still haunts us.

We must face the fact that there are a good many things in our character and in our national life that are inimical to standards—shallowness, complacency, the pursuit of a fast buck, a fondness for short cuts, a willingness to tolerate incompetence, to name only a few.

The importance of competence as a condition of freedom has been widely ignored (as some newly independent nations have found to their sorrow). An amiable fondness for the graces of a free society is not enough. Keeping a free society free—and vital and strong—is no job for the half-educated and the slovenly. Men and women doing capably whatever job is theirs to do tone up the whole society. And those who do a slovenly job, whether they are janitors or judges, surgeons or technicians, lower the tone of the society. So do the chiselers of high and low degree, the sleight-of-hand artists who always know how to gain an advantage without honest work. They are burdens on a free society.

But excellence implies more than competence. It implies a striving for the highest standards in every phase of life. We need individual excellence in all its forms—in every kind of creative endeavor, in politics, in education, in industry, in our spiritual life—in short, universally.

Those who are most deeply devoted to a democratic society must be precisely the ones who insist upon excellence, who insist that free men and women are capable of the highest standards of performance, who insist that a free society can be a great society in the richest sense of that phrase. The idea for which this nation stands will not survive if the highest goal free citizens can set themselves is an amiable mediocrity.

To the extent that we have achieved at least some of our worthiest aims as a nation, we have done so through fierce and faithful effort. Courageous men and women have spent lifetimes of struggle, endurance, and frustration in pursuit of those aims. Others have fought and died for them. And the same measure of devotion is required today. Unlike the great pyramids, the monuments of the spirit will not stand untended. They must be nourished in each generation by the allegiance of believing men and women. Free men and women, in their work, their family life, and in their public behavior should see themselves as builders and maintainers of the values of their society. Individual Americans—bus drivers and editors, grocers and senators, beauty parlor operators and ballplayers—can contribute to the greatness and strength of a free society, or they can help it to die.

It is easy for us to believe that freedom and justice are inexpensive commodities, always there, like the air we breathe, and not things we have to earn, be worthy of, fight for, and cherish. Nothing could be more dangerous to the future of our society. Free men and women must set their own goals. There is no one to tell them what to do; they must do it for themselves. They must be quick to apprehend the kinds of effort and performance their society needs, and they must demand that kind of effort and performance of themselves and of their fellows. They must cherish what Whitehead called "the habitual vision of greatness." If they have the wisdom and courage to demand much of themselves—as individuals and as a society

—they may look forward to long-continued vitality. But a free society that is passive, inert, and preoccupied with its own diversions and comforts will not last long.

As Chesterton put it, "The world will never be safe for democracy—it is a dangerous trade."

But who ever supposed that it would be easy?

Notes

Introduction

1. In *Self-Renewal: The Individual and the Innovative Society* (W.W. Norton, rev. ed., 1981) I deal with various other factors that account for the rise and fall of societies and civilizations.

ONE *The Decline of Hereditary Privilege*

1. R. H. Tawney, *Religion and the Rise of Capitalism*, Penguin Books, Inc., 1947, p. 166.

2. Thomas Jefferson, letter to Roger C. Weightman, June 24, 1826. Adrienne Koch and William Penn (eds.), *The Life and Selected Writings of Thomas Jefferson*, The Modern Library, Random House, 1944, pp. 729–30.

3. In one recent instance, there occurred a head-on collision between the modern aversion to nepotism and an even stronger contemporary value—women's rights. On a good many college campuses there were anti-nepotism rules that prevented, among other things, the hiring of faculty spouses. Such rules were found, under civil rights rulings of the 1970s, to discriminate against women, and were proscribed.

TWO *Individual Achievement versus Equality*

1. Frederick Jackson Turner, *The Frontier in American History*, Henry Holt & Co., Inc., 1920, p. 266.

2. Robert C. Winthrop, "Oration at the Inauguration of the Statue of Benjamin Franklin," Boston, 1836, as quoted in Irvin G. Wyllie, *The Self-Made Man in America*, Rutgers University Press, 1954, pp. 14–15.

3. Alexis de Tocqueville, *Democracy in America* (1840), Alfred A. Knopf, Inc., 1951, Vol. I, p. 249.

4. Henri Herz, "Mes Voyages en Amerique," 1866, in Oscar Handlin, *This Was America*, Harvard University Press, 1949, p. 187.

5. Alistair Cooke, *One Man's America*, Alfred A. Knopf, Inc., 1952.

6. Statements of witnesses before the Ashley Mines Investigation Commission, Parliamentary Papers, 1842.

7. Donald Paterson, "The Conservation of Human Talent," Walter Van Dyke Bingham Lecture, Ohio State University, April 17, 1956.

8. L.A.K.S. Clappe, *The Shirley Letters from the California Mines*, 1851–1852, Alfred A. Knopf, Inc., 1949.

9. Anyone even moderately interested in the subject should read all three: Robert Nozick, *Anarchy, State and Utopia*, Basic Books, 1974; John Rawls, *A Theory of Justice*, Harvard University Press, 1971; Michael Walzer, *Spheres of Justice*, Basic Books, 1983.

10. George Mason in a speech to the Fairfax Independent Company, Alexandria, Virginia, June 1775. Quoted by Perry Miller in *Aspects of Human Equality*, L. Bryson, C. Faust, L. Finklestein, and R. M. MacIver (eds.), Harper & Brothers, 1956, p. 248.

11. G. K. Chesterton, *George Bernard Shaw*, Lane Publishing Co., 1909, p. 215.

12. Aristotle, *Politics*.

13. Lionel Trilling, *The Liberal Imagination*, The Viking Press, 1950, p. 84.

14. Merle Curti, "Intellectuals and Other People," *American Historical Review* 60 no. 2, January 1955, p. 267.

15. Robert Penn Warren, *All the King's Men*, Harcourt, Brace and Company, 1946, p. 101.

16. R. Bretall (ed.), *A Kierkegaard Anthology*, Princeton University Press, 1946, p. 269.

THREE *The Three-Way Contest*

1. I Samuel 22:2.

2. G. B. Shaw, *The Apple Cart*, Penguin Books, Inc., 1956, p. 47.

3. "The Intellectual in the English World," The Listener, October 4, 1956.

FOUR *Civil Rights*

1. James S. Coleman, *Equality of Educational Opportunity*, Government Printing Office, 1966.

FIVE *Equality of Opportunity or Result*

1. John Rawls, *A Theory of Justice*, Harvard University Press, 1971.

2. Ibid.

3. Christopher Jencks et al., *Inequality*, Basic Books, 1972.

SIX *The Great Talent Hunt*

1. "Stanford's Ideal Destiny," Founder's Day address, 1906, *Memories and Studies,* Longmans, Green & Co., 1934.
2. Alfred North Whitehead, *The Aims of Education,* The Macmillan Company, 1929.
3. Irvin G. Wyllie, *The Self-Made Man in America,* Rutgers University Press, 1954, pp. 104–5.
4. Thomas Jefferson, *Notes on the State of Virginia* (1782), William Peden (ed.), University of North Carolina Press, 1955.
5. James S. Coleman, *Equality of Educational Opportunity,* Government Printing Office, 1966.
6. Christopher Jencks, et al., *Inequality,* Basic Books, 1972.

EIGHT *Facts and Fancies about Talent*

1. H. G. Wells, *The Future of America,* Harper and Brothers, 1906, pp. 142–43
2. Consider for example the angry controversy surrounding Arthur Jensen's piece "How Much Can We Boost IQ and Scholarly Achievement," Harvard Educational Review 39 (1969) pp. 1–127.
3. R. L. Atkinson, R. C. Atkinson, and E. R. Hilgard, *Introduction to Psychology* (Eighth Ed.), Harcourt Brace Jovanovich, 1983, p. 374.
4. Catherine M. Cox, et al., *The Early Mental Traits of Three Hundred Geniuses* (Genetic Studies of Genius, Vol. II), Stanford University Press, 1926.
5. Lewis M. Terman, *Genetic Studies of Genius,* Stanford University, 1926.
6. P. S. Sears, "Problems in the Investigation of Achievement and Self-Esteem Motivation," *The Nebraska Symposium on Motivation,* University of Nebraska Press, 1957.
7. Catherine M. Cox, et al., *Early Mental Traits.*
8. I deal with the subject at length in *Self-Renewal,* W. W. Norton, rev. ed. 1981.

NINE *Education as a Sorting-out Process*

1. Roger Barker in a personal letter to the author, 1956.
2. Ibid.
3. Thomas G. Corcoran anecdote in Merle Miller's *Lyndon: An Oral Biography,* G.P. Putnam and Sons, New York, 1980.

TEN *The School's Hard Assignment*

1. Ernest Boyer, *High School: A Report on Secondary Education in America,* Harper & Row, 1983.
2. John Goodlad, *A Place Called School,* McGraw-Hill, 1983.
3. Quoted in *Public Education and the Future of America,* The Educational Policies Commission, 1955, p. 18.
4. National Commission on Excellence in Education, *A Nation at Risk,* Government Printing Office, 1983. See also the Boyer and Goodland studies cited above.

5. John Adams, Letter to John Stebb, September 10, 1785.
6. Fred M. Hechinger, *The New York Times*, October 25, 1983.

ELEVEN *College and the Alternatives*

1. John Rawls, *A Theory of Justice*, Harvard University Press, 1971, p. 81.
2. Ernest Boyer, *High School: A Report on Secondary Education in America*, New York, Harper and Row, 1983, p. 134.
3. Michael Walzer, *Spheres of Justice*, Basic Books, 1983, p. 208.

TWELVE *The Democratic Dilemma*

1. Alfred Lord Tennyson, *Idylls of the King*.
2. Quoted in Richard Hofstadter, *Social Darwinism in American Thought* (rev. ed.), The Beacon Press, 1955, p. 121.
3. Marietta Johnson, *Youth in a World of Men*, The John Day Co., 1929, p. 13.
4. Henri Becque, *Querelles Litteraires*, 1890.
5. Michael Young, *The Rise of the Meritocracy*, 1870–2033, Random House, 1956.
6. Ibid., p. 62.

THIRTEEN *The Full Range of Human Excellence*

1. G.W.E. Russell, *Collections and Recollections*, Harper & Brothers, 1903.
2. Baltasar Gracián, *The Art of Worldy Wisdom*, 1647 (trans. Joseph Jacobs), The Macmillan Company, 1892, p. 12.

FOURTEEN *Lifelong Learning and Growth*

1. Christopher Lloyd, *The Voyages of Captain Cook*, Cresset Press, 1949.

FIFTEEN *Talent and Leadership*

1. For an excellent book-length treatment of the subject, see James McGregor Burns, *Leadership*, Harper and Row, 1978.
2. Thomas Jefferson, letter to George Washington, September 9, 1792, as quoted in Henry A. Washington (ed.), *The Writings of Thomas Jefferson*, Washington, 1853–54, Vol. III, p. 466.
3. Henry James, in a letter to his niece, Catherine James, 1854, as quoted in Ralph Barton Perry, *The Thought and Character of William James*, Vol. I, Little, Brown and Co., 1936, p. 135.
4. Mrs. Humphrey Ward (trans.), *Amiel's Journal*, Macmillan & Co., 1885, pp. 245–46.
5. Thomas Jefferson, letter to John Adams, October 28, 1813, Adrienne Koch and William Penn (eds.), *The Life and Selected Writings of Thomas Jefferson*, The Modern Library, Random House, 1944, p. 633.
6. Chung-li Chang, *The Chinese Gentry*, University of Washington Press, 1955.

SIXTEEN *Leadership and Motivation*

1. Thomas J. Peters and Robert H. Waterman, *In Search of Excellence*, Harper and Row, 1982.
2. Donald Day (ed.), *Uncle Sam's Uncle Josh*, Little, Brown and Co., 1953, p. 169.

SEVENTEEN *The Aims of a Free People*

1. "On Medical Education," from *Science and Education: Essays*, D. Appleton and Company, 1896.
2. Alfred North Whitehad, preface to Wallace B. Donham, *Business Adrift*, Whittlesy House, McGraw-Hill Book Co., Inc., 1931.
3. William Hazlitt, *Lectures on the English Comic Writers*, M. Carey & Son, 1819.
4. "The Social Value of the College Bred," address delivered at Radcliffe College, November 7, 1907, *Memories and Studies*, Longmans, Green & Co., 1934, p. 316.

Index